The Library Reference Series

LIBRARIANSHIP AND LIBRARY RESOURCES

The Library Reference Series

Lee Ash

General Editor

SUBJECT HEADINGS

A Practical Guide

By

DAVID JUDSON HAYKIN

GREGG PRESS

Boston 1972

Library of Congress Cataloging in Publication Data

Haykin, David Judson, 1896-1958.
   Subject headings; a practical guide.

   (Library reference series)
   At head of title: The Library of Congress.
   Reprint of the 1951 ed.
   1. Subject headings. I. United States. Library of
Congress. II. Title.
Z695.H36 1972   025.3'3   72-10141
ISBN 0-8398-0810-0

THE LIBRARY OF CONGRESS

SUBJECT HEADINGS
A Practical Guide

by

DAVID JUDSON HAYKIN

Chief, Subject Cataloging Division

U. S. GOVERNMENT PRINTING OFFICE

WASHINGTON, D. C.

1951

For sale by the Superintendent of Documents, U. S. Government Printing Office
Washington 25, D. C. .   .   .   .   *Price 70 cents*

Table of Contents

Preface

The present guide is intended primarily to satisfy a dual need: first, the recurrent necessity at the Library of Congress of providing trainees in subject cataloging with the rationale and basic rules of practice in the choice and use of subject headings, and, secondly, a necessary basis of common understanding of subject headings for libraries participating in cooperative cataloging.

Principles and rules here stated represent, in considerable part, the views of the catalogers of this country. In particular, they represent the thinking of the staff of subject catalogers at the Library of Congress brought out during weekly and occasional conferences where new headings and old practices are freely discussed. Obviously, present practice deviates at many points from that of the first four decades of this century. It should be borne in mind, too, that subject heading practice at the Library of Congress represents the growth of a half century, during which each cataloger largely followed his own judgment (based on the extent, and the limitations, of his own knowledge of the subject) in establishing and correlating the subject headings in the Library's catalogs. In some instances the stated rule points to a desired change in Library of Congress practice rather than actual usage.

While the guide presents common principles and rules, the wording of the rules and, at times, their interpretation are perforce the work of the writer. In one sense, they are the work of many minds, yet, in another and very real sense, the writer must bear the responsibility for their statement.

Various members of the staff of subject catalogers have assisted in the choice of examples and participated in discussions which provided the groundwork for the formulation of the rules. Since all of them—a number of them no longer at the Library of Congress—have shared in this phase of some of the preparatory work, credit must be given to them collectively. Mrs. Marguerite V. Quattlebaum and Mrs. Barbara Gottschalk Pertzoff assisted substantially in drawing appropriate examples from the catalogs of the Library. Dr. Carl Ginsburg, Dr. Leonard Ellinwood, and Miss Dorothy Norberg shared in the reading of the manuscript and helped substantially in smoothing out many of the rough places in the language of the text and in securing consistency in matters of style. Mr. Herman H. Henkle and Dr. Frederick H. Wagman, successively directors of the Processing Department, were generous in constructive criticism and in securing for the writer leave from his regular duties in order to prepare the guide. Special expression of gratitude is due to Mr. Leo E. LaMontagne, Deputy Chief of the Subject Cataloging Division and its Principal Cataloger, for taking over the responsibility of the Division's administration, during a period of great pressure of work, in addition to his regular duties.

DAVID JUDSON HAYKIN.

I. Introduction

For the purposes of this work it is unnecessary to go into the history of subject catalogs at length. It is important, however, to distinguish clearly other types of subject catalogs from the modern alphabetical subject catalog.

The alphabetical subject catalog, either self-contained, or as the subject element in the dictionary catalog, is a later development than the systematic, or classed, catalog (*Realkatalog, catalogue raisonné*). In this country it has almost completely displaced the latter. The principal classed catalogs now remaining are those of the Engineering Societies Library in New York, the John Crerar Library in Chicago, and the Science and Technology Department of the Carnegie Library of Pittsburgh. There are, nevertheless, many things to commend the classed catalog. Rudolf Kaiser [1] sums up the argument between the classed and the dictionary catalog by stating that a library needs both and explaining that the subject index fills the need as far as an alphabetical catalog is concerned. However, his conclusion misses the mark, since, for one not completely the master of the system of classification, there is no approach to the classed catalog save through an index, yet the index is not in fact as complete and direct a guide to the subject content of the library's collections as an alphabetical catalog rationally and fully cross-referenced.

Failure to appraise fairly the respective virtues of the classed and the alphabetical subject catalog rests, in part at least, on a misapprehension of the primary functions of classification and subject headings. Proponents of the classed catalog maintain that the alphabetical catalog cannot replace the classed catalog since it scatters individual concepts in such a way that related concepts can be brought together only through an extensive grouping of headings by means of subdivision—a procedure which violates the basic principles of subject headings. As a matter of fact, the primary purpose of the subject catalog is to show which books on a specific subject the library possesses. Its use as a source of general subject bibliography—a use which is a partial justification of the classed catalog— is of secondary importance. The functions of classification, on the other hand, are: 1) to arrange books on the shelves so that similar works will stand together and related books adjacent to them; and 2) to provide a convenient basis for symbols to make it possible to go directly to the desired books and to replace them correctly on the shelf.

To use a system of classification as a means of finding all books on a particular subject one would have to resort to an alphabetical index. Where a subject possesses several aspects which must be separated in a given system of classifica-

---

[1] Fritz Milkau, ed. *Handbuch der Bibliothekswissenschaft* (1931–40), II, 299–300.

tion, *e. g.*, the economic aspects of railway transportation as distinguished from railroad engineering, a relative index is needed which will show under each entry the different senses in which the term is used and the diverse aspects of the subject with their appropriate places in the classification system. Where a book treats of two or more topics, an index to the classification is of no use in finding any topic other than the one by which the book is classified, but a classed catalog, as distinguished from the system of classification, provides for multiple entry for the same work in a manner corresponding to that of the alphabetical subject catalog. An alphabetical index is inevitable, since otherwise only a complete knowledge of the interrelation of broad and specific topics would permit the user of the catalog to find the topic of his interest.

Because of this necessity of an index and probably also because of the aversion of most library users for symbols they do not readily understand, the alphabetical subject catalog, using verbal headings rather than symbols, has displaced the classed catalog in most American libraries. The fact that natural scientists do not react as unfavorably to symbols as do specialists in the humanities and social sciences may account in part for the survival of the classed catalog in the three scientific libraries named above. From these remarks it should not be inferred that the classed catalog does not possess substantial advantages over the alphabetical catalog. If a balance were struck, after all logical and practical considerations are taken into account, the classed catalog might very well prove to be the more economical and useful. For our purpose, however, the principal consideration is the fact that the alphabetical catalog has generally found favor with the type of readers served by most American libraries, be they public, school, or university libraries.

A catalog which uses verbal subject headings to enable readers to find material on broad or specific topics directly, without requiring reference to an index, obviously lacks the advantage of the classed catalog in bringing all of the material on a given subject together and arranging it on the basis of its logical interrelationships. The alphabetical catalog can make up for this lack in part by its syndetic apparatus, that is, the system of references between related subjects. For a reader who desires material on all aspects of a given subject, its pursuit through the catalog by means of references is admittedly a long process, which in a classed catalog is on the whole unnecessary. Comprehensive searches of this sort, however, occur but rarely. In most instances, a reader either seeks material on a particular topic or desires a treatise on the broad subject. For this purpose the alphabetical subject catalog is wholly adequate, since the reader need look in the catalog only under the precise topic he seeks.

The alphabetico-classed catalog, which had some vogue in American libraries prior to the dominance of the dictionary catalog, represents an attempt to combine some of the advantages of a classed catalog with the directness and ease of consultation of the alphabetical subject catalog of the present day. Its entries were names of broad subjects alphabetically arranged, each followed by a topic of the next order of comprehensiveness, further subdivided if necessary by a still lower order. Under each heading in the alphabet of broad subject headings there was an alphabetic arrangement of topics, and under some of the topics a further subarrangement. The grouping of topics resembled the classed catalog, with the important difference that the broad subjects themselves were in alphabetic rather than systematic order and the topics under each were again arranged alphabetically, not on the basis of their relationships. The advantage of grouping topics under the broader subject is reduced by the need to make references from the specific topic and its synonyms to the echelon of subjects of which it is the last member. C. A. Cutter [2] illustrates the difference between the subject headings of a dictionary catalog (which includes the alphabetical subject catalog) and the alphabetico-classed catalog by pointing out that the alphabetico-classed catalog enters works on the life of Napoleon under *Biography* and a history of England under *History*, whereas a dictionary catalog enters them under *Napoleon* and *England* respectively. A more striking example, perhaps, is the dictionary catalog heading *Frogs* for which the corresponding alphabetico-classed heading would presumably be *Zoology* [or *Animal kingdom*]—*Vertebrates*—*Amphibians*—*Frogs*, which still does not represent all of the stages in the zoological classification of frogs. Each step in the echelon and its synonyms would require a reference on the order of the following:

> Frogs
> >*see*
> Zoology [or Animal kingdom]—Vertebrates—Amphibians—Frogs

> Amphibians
> >*see*
> Zoology [or Animal kingdom]—Vertebrates—Amphibians

> Vertebrates
> >*see*
> Zoology [or Animal kingdom]—Vertebrates

One should note, however, that many topics, no matter how specific, would be entered in the alphabetico-classed catalog directly under the topic, as in the dictionary catalog, especially in the case of topics whose class relationships are not obvious or common, as *Ink*, *Lace*, *Leather*, *Salt*, or *Varnish*. On the other hand, dictionary catalogs have not always avoided headings of the alphabetico-classed type, *e. g.*, *English language—Verb*. To use the specific term *English verb* would separate it from other aspects of the English language.

In effect the headings for a given topic in an alphabetico-classed and a dictionary catalog are equally specific. The difference lies in the fact that in the former the specific topic is the last element in a complex heading, whereas in the

---

[2] Charles A. Cutter, *Rules for a Dictionary Catalogue* (3d ed.; 1891), p. 12.

latter it is named directly; what distinguishes the subject heading in a present-day dictionary catalog from other forms is that it is both specific and direct.[3]

While the subject catalog has almost completely displaced all other forms in this country, it nevertheless suffers from several limitations, some accidental, others inherent in its nature and structure. Whatever rules or principles were applied in choosing or devising headings in the past, it is clear that they were often based on no more than the limited personal experience of the cataloger. One of the most serious weaknesses of the headings now found in our catalogs is that the terms chosen are not derived from precise knowledge of the approach used by many readers of different backgrounds.

Naturally, the term applied to an object or idea will vary with the age and background of the user, his special knowledge of the subject field, his occupation, the geographic area in which he lives and works—in general, his cultural milieu. In public libraries, which have to serve a diversified clientele, the problem of the choice of terms involves finding a common denominator which would meet the needs of the majority, or the more important part, of its public. The only problem which a public library does not have to meet is that of regional or geographic differences; even so, the problem is not completely absent in the case of libraries in large centers with a fluid population. Solution is sometimes reached by taking account of the lower intellectual levels of the population; in cities with dominant industries or occupations, the language of the industry or occupation is adopted for its subject field, other factors being applied to the choice of headings in other fields.

Choice of terms is, however, only one of the factors in making the catalog a fully effective tool for different categories of readers. Other factors represent a kind of no man's land. Very little by way of objective, experimental data is available on the general approach of the reader to the subject element of the dictionary catalog. There is little evidence to show what proportion of the users of the catalog employ it to find books by subject and how that proportion varies with different categories of readers and libraries. No valid data exist to show whether readers, and what categories of readers, seek books under a specific heading or a comprehensive subject.[4] Further, we need to know how the reader is affected by the internal structure of subject headings—types of subdivision, methods of qualification. Possibly of secondary importance are the following problems: 1) the advantages and disadvantages of headings of the alphabetico-classed type; 2) the relative merits of popular and scientific names, especially of popular English and foreign scientific names; and 3) the best position of references to related subjects with respect to the heading from which the references are made,

---

[3] For the purposes of this work, the term "specific," when applied to a subject heading, will be used in this sense of "both specific and direct" and the term "subject catalog" in the sense either of an alphabetical subject catalog based on such subject headings, or the subject element of a modern dictionary catalog.

[4] A study of this factor might, incidentally, assist encyclopedists to determine whether articles should combine specific topics under broad subjects or treat them individually.

that is, whether preceding the heading and its subdivisions, or following the simple heading but preceding the subdivisions, or following the heading and all its subdivisions.[5]

Even if the cataloger were to determine conclusively the mental processes of the reader and to choose the terms, structure, and arrangement of headings which most closely correspond to the reader's approach, he would still have to take account of linguistic problems. A school child would conceivably seek a book on the history of the United States under the heading *American history* or *America— History*, not being aware that "America" is to the educated adult a more inclusive term than "United States." To a physician the term "icterus" may be intelligible, although an American physician is likely to look for material on the subject under the heading *Jaundice;* only the latter would have any meaning to a layman. Other factors bearing on the language of the heading are homonyms and semantic changes. The term "labor" has a different meaning to the obstetrician than to the economist, and "icterus," which means "jaundice" to a physician, means "oriole" to an ornithologist. Semantic changes cause the cataloger to use a term in current usage rather than an outmoded one which is nevertheless used by the authors of the work to be cataloged; the cataloger must be constantly aware of change and bring the catalog up-to-date by changing headings which have gone out of use. This is illustrated by the succession *Domestic economy*, *Domestic science*, and *Home economics*, the first of which was in use before the turn of the century, the second before World War I, and the third of which appeared about the turn of the century and is now the term in general use, finding some competition, however, in the terms "homemaking" and "household arts" (or "science").

A semantic problem with which catalogers must struggle constantly is that of imperfect synonyms. Scientific terms are, generally speaking, quite precise in their meanings; in other fields of knowledge and in the use of popular terms, which may be preferred to scientific terms in certain instances, meanings are inexact, the same term being used in different senses by different categories of readers or in different regions, just as different terms are applied to the same thing. "Crocodiles" and "alligators," for example, are terms which are interchangeable in popular usage, whereas in scientific usage the two genera are distinct.

The present work offers solutions, however imperfect, of the problems of reader approach, of semantics, of verbal structure or morphology, and of coordination, in order that the work of catalogers may present as much consistency and uniformity as possible, particularly necessary where cataloging is carried on cooperatively by libraries which are widely dispersed. As further experience and objective study show principles and rules of practice to be faulty or inadequate, they will be displaced or modified. Meanwhile, the statements which are embodied in the following chapters represent the most valid current practice as

---

[5] In Library of Congress practice, the references are placed following the simple heading, but before its subdivisions.

evolved in the Library of Congress and the libraries which voluntarily follow it. The subject headings now in use in the dictionary catalogs of the Library of Congress represent fifty years' growth. Many of them were valid and well chosen at the time of their adoption. They have remained unchanged because the need for change did not appear urgent or because the cost, in the light of more urgent needs, made change inexpedient. The principles and rules of practice here presented represent, in many instances, what is desirable, rather than what has actually been achieved.

II. Fundamental Concepts

Some indication of the problems affecting the choice of terminology was given in the Introduction. As was brought out there, it is obvious that, in the face of a lack of sufficient objective, experimental data, we must rely for guidance in the choice of terms upon the experience of librarians and such objective findings as are available, insofar as they appear to be conclusive and practical, for formulating the principles upon which the choice must rest.

The Reader as the Focus. The reference to our lack of knowledge in regard to the approach of various classes and categories of readers to the subject catalog clearly points to the fundamental principle that the reader is the focus in all cataloging principles and practice. All other considerations, such as convenience and the desire to arrange entries in some logical order, are secondary to the basic rule that the heading, in wording and structure, should be that which the reader will seek in the catalog, if we know or can presume what the reader will look under. To the extent that the headings represent the predilection of the cataloger in regard to terminology and are dictated by conformity to a chosen logical pattern, as against the likely approach of the reader resting on psychological rather than logical grounds, the subject catalog will lose in effectiveness and ease of approach, since at best the reader would find a reference to the heading he seeks, rather than the heading itself.

Accepting the above principle as a cataloging axiom, the fundamental rules are, broadly speaking, inevitable results of the experience of librarians in meeting the demands of readers who seek material on particular topics. As far as possible, these rules should provide a direct approach to the topic for most of the clientele of the library, references serving the needs of minorities among readers and suggesting to the reader the way to further or more direct search.

Unity. A subject catalog must bring together under one heading all the books which deal principally or exclusively with the subject, whatever the terms applied to it by the authors of the books and whatever the varying terms applied to it at different times. The cataloger must, therefore, choose with care the term to be used and apply it uniformly to all the books on the subject. He must choose a term which is unambiguous and does not overlap in meaning other headings in the catalog, even where that involves defining the sense in which it is used as compared with, or distinguished from, other closely related headings. Obviously, the cataloger must guide the reader who might be more familiar with other synonymous terms by making references from all synonyms.[1] As a corol-

---

[1] The method of making such references is treated in the chapter on the structure and integration of the catalog.

lary, the same term must not be used for more than one subject. If a term is used in more than one sense, as when it is used in more than one field of knowledge, it must be qualified in such a way that the reader will know precisely which meaning to attach to the term.

Usage. The heading chosen must represent common usage or, at any rate, the usage of the class of reader for whom the material on the subject within which the heading falls is intended. Usage in an American library must inevitably mean current American usage. Unless this principle is adhered to faithfully most readers will not find the material they desire under the heading which first occurs to them, if they find it at all. "Icterus," for example, may be a familiar term to medical men, particularly to continental European medical men; nevertheless, American writers and readers use almost exclusively the popular term "jaundice," hence, the obvious choice for the catalog is *Jaundice.* By the same token, a contemporary term is to be used, and not one the use of which has declined. A case in point is "consumption" in the sense of pulmonary tuberculosis. At the turn of the century and after, "consumption" was the popular term and was in general use in publications in the field of public health; "phthisis" in that sense had already gone out of use. Yet, clearly, "tuberculosis" is the prevalent, commonly understood term now, used both by laymen and in medical literature.

This brings us to the consideration of semantic change as it affects the catalog. The cataloger who is constantly in contact with the literature of his special subject becomes aware of changes in meaning as they occur. These he must incorporate into the subject catalog. He must use the term in the sense in which it is currently used, regardless of the older literature in and out of the catalog. This leads inevitably to a policy of constant change in order to maintain the catalog up to date. To put this policy into effect the cataloger must substitute the latest heading for the one which is obsolescent or obsolete and must refer the reader to the current heading from the headings which have fallen into disuse. Old headings may be retained when it is inexpedient to change, in which case references must be made from the current term known to most readers to the old one in the catalog. The result of such a procedure, obviously, is that readers do not have direct access to the heading they are most likely to look for.

The implication which cannot be avoided is that general dictionaries of American English, as well as dictionaries in particular subject fields, are not to be used as the source of headings, unless the latest and most commonly used term is selected. Dictionaries record both older terms no longer in use and terms in use at the time of the compilation of the dictionary. They do not usually indicate a choice on the basis of currency. The surest sources of usage are periodicals on various subjects. If there is agreement on terms among those contemporaries who have competence in the subject and write on it for others, including readers of like competence, it is safe to use such terms. Where there is diversity among the writers, the choice must fall on the term most often used, provided the cataloger keeps in mind the kind of reader the library serves, his social background and intellectual level.

Whether a popular term or a scientific one is to be chosen depends on several considerations. If the library serves a miscellaneous public, it must prefer the popular to the scientific term. It may even prefer it, if the popular term is commonly used in the professional or scientific literature; in speaking of the genus bee in general, for example, even the scientist will use the term "bee" rather than *Apis*. However, the popular term must be precise and unambiguous; thus, "crab grass" would not be a desirable term to use as a heading, since it is used in different senses in different parts of the country and both for grasses and for the glasswort, which is supposed to be the food of crabs. On the other hand, in a zoological library or a collection limited, say, to *Hymenoptera*, it would be proper to use the scientific term *Apis*, in order to bring together material on the genus and the several species.

English vs. Foreign Terms. Foreign terms should be used only under the following conditions: 1) when the concept is foreign to Anglo-American experience and no satisfactory term for it exists, *e. g., Reallast, Précieuses;* and 2) when, especially in the case of scientific names, the foreign term is precise, whereas the English one is not, *e. g., Ophiodon elongatus*, rather than *Buffalo cod*, or *Blue cod*; *Pityrosporum ovale*, rather than *Bottle bacillus.* Terms of foreign origin, which retain their foreign form, but which have been incorporated into the English vocabulary are, of course, to be regarded as English words, *e. g., Terrazzo, Sauerkraut.*

Specificity. The heading should be as specific as the topic it is intended to cover. As a corollary, the heading should not be broader than the topic; rather than use a broader heading, the cataloger should use two specific headings which will approximately cover it.

This principle of specificity is applicable also to headings in an alphabetico-classed catalog. In a dictionary catalog or a separate alphabetical subject catalog employing subject headings in the present-day sense, the headings are not merely specific, but are both direct and specific, naming the topic without the interposition of the broader subject.

The argument for the directly specific as against the alphabetico-classed heading has been presented earlier. It is necessary, however, to state the reason for the use of the most specific heading applicable, rather than the broader heading which comprehends it.

If the subject catalog were to consist of a predetermined number of more or less broad headings, a work on a specific topic would have to be entered under the broader one. The broader heading would thus be used for works as comprehensive as the heading, as well as for works on all the topics comprehended by it. To find out whether the library possesses a book on a specific topic, the reader would, in the first place, need to know how broad a heading might be used for it, and, in the second place, would have to scan all the entries under the broader heading in order to select those which are of interest to him.   Even then, he would be able to identify only those of which the titles clearly indicate the subject; conceivably the titles might be cryptic, even misleading.   This may be illustrated as follows: a reader looking for material on the income tax can be sure of finding it quickly and surely only by looking under the heading *Income tax*.   If the library were to choose a broader heading, it would have to be *Taxation* or even *Finance, Public*. Obviously, the number of entries under either would be relatively large in any library.   The reader could not, in any case, be certain that he had hit upon the heading which the library has, more or less arbitrarily, chosen for topics related to and including the income tax, even after he had scanned all the entries under the above two.   If the titles failed to mention the income tax by this very term or by a recognizable synonym of it, they would be lost to the reader.   How could the reader suspect, for example, that *The Real Single Tax* by Christian Botker is wholly devoted to the income tax, rather than to the single tax?

It may be admitted that readers do not necessarily seek material under the most specific heading.   In the writer's experience, a reader who, as it turned out, wanted material on canaries asked for books about birds.   It is impossible to make certain that the reader will find precisely what he wants with the minimum effort unless the headings are specific.   For the one who seeks specific information under a broad heading, references from the broad to specific headings subordinate to it, on which the library has material, will either guide the reader to the particular heading he wants or suggest to him that he should look under a specific heading to find material on a specific topic.

How specific should the headings be?   As stated above, it is virtually impossible to set a standard for the breadth of a heading, if a specific one is not to be used.   If it were desired to use a broader heading than *Canaries* for books about canaries, would it be: *Finches*, to which family the canary belongs (or *Fringillidae*, the scientific name of this family); *Oscines* (or *Singing birds*),[2] the suborder; *Passeriformes*, the order; or *Cagebirds*, reflecting the use of these birds?   There are limits to the principle of specificity, however, beyond which its application does not appear to serve the best interests of the reader.   For example, to provide for material on raw silk, in any but a textile library, under *Raw silk* would separate it from very closely related material on other forms of silk; even *Silk, Raw* would be some distance away in the catalog from *Silk*, since it would follow all the subdivisions under the heading *Silk*.   In view of the absence of objective findings on the approach of the reader to the subject headings in the catalog, the limits of specificity must, therefore, be based in the first place on experience in helping readers to find books on various subjects.   Beyond that, there are the limits which are inherent in language itself and in the form of the headings.

It is safe to assume that the reader who seeks material on a particular person, corporate body, object, event, and the like, will look under some form of the

---

[2] The Library of Congress has found no occasion to use *Oscines*, although the others have been used for books to which they were appropriate.

proper name, although it is not outside the realm of probability that some reader will look under a generic term comprehending the particular name. Thus, books on Thomas Jefferson, Harvard University, the Taj Mahal, the Battle of Bunker Hill are likely to be sought under the headings: *Jefferson, Thomas*, rather than *Presidents—U. S.; Harvard University*, rather than *Universities—U. S.; Taj Mahal*, rather than, though possibly, *Architecture, Oriental* or *Architecture—Agra; Bunker Hill, Battle of, 1775*, rather than, but also, conceivably, *Battles* or *U. S.—History—Revolution*.

It is unlikely that the reader will look under an adjective denoting language, ethnic group, or place for material on a subject limited by language, ethnic group, or place, although, in the case of ethnic groups particularly, the interest in the group may outweigh that in the subject. On this basis it has been assumed, although it has not been demonstrated, that a reader interested in French art or French anonyms and pseudonyms would be much more likely to look under *Art, French* (or *Art—France*) and *Anonyms and pseudonyms, French* than under the respective uninverted forms, that is, the linguistic, ethnic, or local adjective, which may be considered the more specific approach to the subject.

Where the specific term denotes a variety rather than a species, as, for example, in names of makes of automobiles or machinery, it is questionable whether the reader would look under the specific term; hence, the name of the species followed, if necessary, by the name of the variety is likely to be the better choice of heading. This would not be applicable in a special library or in one which had a large collection of material on the subject. Thus, *Automobiles* is adequate for all makes and types, especially when used with subdivisions such as *Lubrication, Repairing, Apparatus and supplies*. It is, nevertheless, not unreasonable, at the same time, to single out *Ford automobile*, either because of the number of books on the subject, or because it may be considered a species, or special type, of automobile. In an automotive library it would probably be desirable to use special headings also for the Packard automobile or even the Ford motor truck.

As a general rule, however, when a term sanctioned by American usage is available for an object (or group of objects), a concept, or a relationship, it may be used as a subject heading. Under this principle there is justification for such specific headings as *Autumn, Quatrain, Ultrafax, Waltz*.

In fine, a subject heading used in the modern dictionary catalog or alphabetical subject catalog represents a choice of that term to designate the subject which is to be used consistently regardless of the language of the author. This term must, if possible, be sanctioned by current American usage. It must not be any broader than the subject matter of the books to which the heading is assigned.

892869—51——2

III. Structure and Integration of the Subject Catalog

The subject element of the dictionary catalog includes the following types of entries: subject and form headings, references from synonymous terms not intended to be used as subject headings to the heading chosen in lieu of them, references from broad comprehensive headings to specific and subordinate headings and from both broad and specific headings to other related headings of the same order of comprehensiveness, general references to groups or classes of headings, references from subject headings to names of personal and corporate authors, to anonymous classics, and to class numbers in the shelflist, and finally scope notes.

"See" References. Given a subject heading chosen in accordance with stated principles, but above all because it is a term commonly used by writers on the subject and is most likely to be known to the reader interested in the subject, the heading is used without deviation for books on that subject, regardless of the term applied to it by the author of a particular book. Thus, the heading brings together all books dealing comprehensively with the subject represented by the heading. However, since other terms exist or have been used in books, periodical articles, or essays on the subject, and since these terms are likely to be known—might, in fact, be better known—to some reader, it stands to reason that the reader must be directed from the term he looks under in the catalog to the one chosen. This type of reference is known as a "see" reference. It tells the reader something like this: "That which you seek under this heading is to be found in this catalog under the heading referred to," or "Look for the subject matter you desire under the heading referred to," *e. g.,*

> Ex-service men
> *see*
> Veterans

> Consumption
> *see*
> Tuberculosis

> Phthisis
> *see*
> Tuberculosis

A "see" reference is often made from other than synonymous terms. In fact, its basic significance is that the subject matter is entered not under the heading which occurred to the reader, but under the one chosen by the cataloger even when the terms are not completely synonymous. The following are examples of such a "see" reference:

> Early printed books
> *see*
> Bibliography—Early printed books—16th century
> Bibliography—Rare books
> Incunabula
>
> Farm animals
> *see*
> Domestic animals
> Stock and stock-breeding
>
> Ministers (Diplomatic agents)
> *see*
> Ambassadors
> Diplomatic and consular service

"See also" References. It is supposed that the alphabetical subject catalog leaves logic out of consideration in the arrangement of topics. Its alphabetic order has been the feature most widely criticized. Ranganathan, who has gone further than anyone else in introducing order and logic into librarianship,[1] speaks of the arrangement of entries in the alphabetical subject catalog as "artificial scattering" and recommends the adoption of the classed catalog as the new form (*sic!*) in place of the "old respected Dictionary Catalogue."[2] However, there are in the dictionary catalog certain substitutes for logic, devices which bring related material together. At this point our interest is limited to only one of these devices, the system of "see also" references, which bind related headings together. It is this feature of the catalog which has led Cutter and his successors to call the alphabetical subject aspect of the dictionary catalog "syndetic."

In binding related headings together the basic rule is that a "see also" reference be made from a given subject: 1) to more specific subjects or topics comprehended within it, or to an application of the subject; and 2) to coordinate subjects which suggest themselves as likely to be of interest to the user seeking material under the given heading, because they represent other aspects of the subject, or are closely related to it. The suggestive element of the heading is important in that the reader may not be fully aware of the scope of the heading he is looking

---

[1] This is evidenced primarily by his *The Five Laws of Library Science* (Madras, 1931), *Colon Classification* (1933), *Classified Catalogue Code* (1934), *Prolegomena to Library Classification* (1937), and *Theory of Library Catalogue* (1938).

[2] *Theory of Library Catalogue*, p. 179 ff.

under.   The material of first interest to him may in fact be under another heading, one of those to which a reference has been made.   The reference thus makes him aware of the heading under which he will find the material he wants.

General References.   "See also" references are usually directed to particular headings to be found in the catalog.   When so used they are called specific references.   Frequently, however, when the headings to be referred to are obviously individual members of a single class or category, the reference is made not to the individual members but to the class, and several members are added by way of example.   Such a "see also" reference is called a general reference.

It may well be argued that general references defeat the syndetic aspect of an alphabetic subject catalog in that the specific subject headings to which the reference should lead are not all named, but are represented merely by an example. It is, however, unlikely that any but an occasional reader would seek all the material in the library covered by all the specific headings comprehended by the broad one from which the general reference is made.   If he should, he would be wiser to seek his material through bibliographies, or to refer to systematic treatises on the broad subject for the topics for which there would be headings in the catalog should the library possess separate works on them.   The purpose of the general reference is primarily suggestive.   It suggests the pattern of the headings under which a particular class or group of topics is entered.   In so doing, it makes it possible for the reader to find the material he seeks under any or—with the aid of systematic works on the general subject—all of the topics covered by headings of this pattern.   Frequently, a reader will look for material on a specific topic under a broad heading simply because he is unaware of the principle of specific entry used in the catalog.   To him the general reference offers the hint that he should look under the heading covering the specific topic.   The general reference below, under *Birds*, would suggest *Canaries* to him, if he were looking under *Birds* for material on canaries.   Examples of general references:

> Birds.
> *See also names of different kinds of birds, e. g.,* Humming birds;
> Plovers; Terns.

> Civilian defense.
> *See also subdivision* Civilian defense *under names of countries, cities, etc., e. g.,* Gt. Brit.—Civilian defense.

> Consumer education.
> *See also specific consumer problems, e. g.,* Food adulteration
> and inspection; Instalment plan; Labels.

General references do not stand alone but are combined with specific references, being placed at the end of the list of specific headings referred to.   There are at least two reasons why general references are placed at the end: 1) the examples cited may need to be changed or added to; and 2) the specific references are ordinarily arranged in alphabetic order while general references cannot be.

In a small library, where the number of specific headings in the catalog is small, it is obviously unnecessary to use general references. In a larger library, however, a distinct advantage results from their use: they obviate the need of long lists of specific headings, thus saving space in the catalog; they also bring to the attention of the reader the most direct method of finding the material he desires and accomplish it by a brief statement accompanied by examples.

While "see" references to a given heading adopted for use in the catalog should be made from all synonymous and variant English terms found in the literature of the subject, except when they would stand in the catalog next to each other or to the heading referred to, "see also" references are obviously to be made only between headings actually in the catalog. Subject headings are adopted for and used in the catalog as the need for them arises, that is, as books requiring them are cataloged. The system of references which binds subjects together is, consequently, as complete, and only as complete, as the headings in actual use permit.

References to Names of Authors and to Anonymous Classics. References from subject headings to names of individuals and corporate bodies and to headings used for anonymous classics [3] are made primarily as a measure of economy of space in the catalog. The practice is fully justified from the point of view of convenience to the reader. It avoids the multiplication of subject entries in instances where the author, or inevitable added entries, are sufficient to bring the material to the attention of the reader. Such references to names of individuals are indicated from headings designating occupations, for example:

> Architects, British
> *see also*
> **Wren,** *Sir* **Christopher, 1632–1723**
>
> Scientists, Arabic
> *see also*
> **Avicenna, 980?–1037**
>
> Economists, American
> *see also*
> **Veblen, Thorstein, 1857–1929**
> **Walker, Francis Amasa, 1840–1897**

---

[3] Because in many libraries subject headings are written in red ink, other headings are referred to in contradistinction to subject headings as "black headings" and references from subject headings to them as "references to black headings." The Library of Congress and many other libraries write or print subject headings in capital letters, hence these terms are no longer applicable.

> Painters, French
>   *see also*
> **Bonheur, Rosa, 1822–1899**
> **Matisse, Henri, 1869–**
> **Meissonier, Jean Louis Ernest, 1815–1891**

While the names referred to are used both as author and as subject headings, and the reference is primarily intended to lead the reader to the heading used as subject, it is at the same time the only guide to autobiographical material for which many libraries do not use the name of the autobiographer as a subject heading.

A reference from the subject heading for a particular kind of society or institution should be made to the names of individual societies of that kind as a guide to such of their publications as describe their purposes, activities, history, and proceedings. This obviates the necessity of using the subject heading designating the kind of society or institution for every entry of this character. It is exactly parallel with the use of the reference from the name of the occupation to the names of individuals who follow that occupation for the purpose of guiding the reader to autobiographical material. The following are cited as examples:

> Medicine—Societies
>   *see also*
> **Academy of Medicine of Cincinnati**
> **Colorado State Medical Society**
> **Medical Women's International Association**

> Women as physicians
>   *see also*
> **Medical Women's International Association**

> Agricultural experiment stations—France
>   *see also*
> **Beauvais.   Station agronomique**

> Prisons—U. S.
>   *see also*
> **U.S.** *Federal Industrial Institution for Women, Alderson, W.Va.*
> **U.S.** *Northeastern Penitentiary, Lewisburg, Pa.*
> **U.S.** *Penitentiary, Atlanta*

As a corollary to this rule, publications of a society or institution which are not solely descriptive of it or an account of its activities, but which contain contributions to knowledge in the field of its interest, require a subject heading under the name of the field of interest with the subdivision *Societies, etc.* The subdivision in this case serves to separate publications of societies and institutions from general treatises on the subject, periodicals, etc.

Similarly, references from appropriate subject headings are made to names of individual anonymous classics, for example:

> Epic poetry
> *see also*
> **Chanson de Roland**
> **Kalevala**
> **Nibelungenlied**
>
> Romances
> *see also*
> **Alexander the Great** (*Romances, etc.*)
> **Arthur, King** (*Romances, etc.*)
> **Guy of Warwick** (*Romance*)
> **Örvar-Odds saga**
>
> Hebrew literature
> *see also*
> **Midrash**
> **Talmud**

References like the above should be made from the most specific subject headings applicable in each instance, on the same grounds as references from any subject heading to subordinate or more specific headings. It may sometimes be necessary to refer from more than one subject heading to the same author heading, as in the case of **Medical Women's International Association** above.

Scope Notes. An important element in helping the reader orient himself in the catalog are the scope notes. They may be defined as statements which indicate the subject matter covered by a given heading, usually with reference to related, more particularly, overlapping headings. It partakes of the nature of a definition on the one hand and a "see also" reference on the other. It may, in fact, include both definitions and references. Its principal feature, however, is that it indicates the limits within which the subject entries under it fall and at what points other headings will serve the reader's needs.

An example of a simple scope note, unencumbered by distinctions or references of any kind, is the following:

> Education, Cooperative.
> > Here are entered works dealing with the plan of instruction under which students spend alternating periods in school and in a practical occupation.

The term "cooperative education" does not make clear the sense in which it is used; neither do such of its synonyms as "study-work plan," "work-study plan," "work experience in education." For that reason a scope note is necessary.

The scope note for the heading *Industrial relations* illustrates the type which includes references to specific related subjects:

> Industrial relations.
>
>> Here are entered works dealing with employer-employee relations in general. For special aspects of this relationship, *e. g.*, Arbitration, Industrial; Collective bargaining; Employees' representation in management, etc., *see* those specific subjects. For the legal aspects of industrial relations *see* Labor laws and legislation. For the technique of personnel management and relations from the employers' point of view *see* Employment management. For works descriptive of the social and economic conditions of labor *see* Labor and laboring classes.

The scope note which embodies a general reference is illustrated by the following:

> Commodity exchanges.
>
>> Here are entered works on commodity exchanges in general. For works on exchanges dealing in a single commodity or class of commodities, *e. g.*, cotton, grain, tobacco, *see* Cotton trade, Grain trade, etc.

In general, a scope note is necessary when general dictionaries and dictionaries in special subjects fail to agree completely, and when usage does not offer a sufficiently precise definition of the subject. Under these circumstances, it limits the scope of the subject as used in the catalog, thereby helping the reader to determine to what extent the heading covers the material he seeks and making it possible for the cataloger to maintain consistency in the assignment of the subject heading.

Coordination of Reference Structure. The syndetic and coordinating character of the system of headings and references is illustrated by the heading *Civilian defense*, which happens to require all of the types of references described.

Civilian defense is the heading used for works dealing with military and related measures for the protection and defense of the civilian population, without reference to country, or applicable to all, or to several, countries. In the literature of the subject the term "civil defense" is also used; therefore, a "see" reference is indicated from *Civil defense*. This reference would not be needed if the catalog did not contain: 1) such headings as *Civil engineering, Civil law, Civil rights*; and, in the case of a dictionary catalog, 2) such names of corporate bodies as **Civil Disobedience Enquiry Committee** and **Civil Liberties Committee of Massachusetts,** or references to names of corporate bodies established in the catalog from former or variant forms of the names, as, for example, **Civil Engineers' Club of Cleveland** and **Civilian Conservation Corps;** 3) main and secondary entries under title, such as *Civil service bulletin, Civil journey, Civil wrongs and their legal remedies;* and 4) pseudonyms like **Civilian.** All of these follow

Civil defense, the heading referred from, and precede *Civilian defense*, the heading used and, therefore, the one to which the reference directs the reader.[4]

Because some readers are likely to think of the term "civilian" or "civil" in this connection simply as one which defines and modifies the term "defense," a reference is indicated from the inverted form, *Defense, Civil*. A further reference from *Defense, Civilian* should not be made, since it would follow immediately after the reference from *Defense, Civil*.

The broad subject within which civilian defense falls and from which a reference has to be made is *Military art and science*. Reference is also made from *Attack and defense (Military science)*, because civilian defense is an aspect of military defense, for which the latter heading is intended, even though it is not clearly or fully comprehended within it.

From *Civilian defense*, in turn, "see also" references are made to *Air defenses*, a heading coordinate with it and partly comprehended within it, as well as to the following headings for phases of civilian defense: *Air raid shelters; Decontamination (from gases, chemicals, etc.); World War, 1939–1945—Evacuation of civilians*.

Civilian defense is used for works dealing with the principles, general aspect, and applications of the subject without reference to a particular geographic area or political jurisdiction, or with reference to several countries, in comparing their methods, laws, etc. However, if a work is limited to the discussion of laws, regulations, methods, and procedures applicable in one country alone, the heading used consists of the name of the country, state, or city followed by the subdivision *Civilian defense*. Obviously, a reference is required from the broad heading *Civilian defense* to the names of the geographic areas and political jurisdictions under which the subdivision *Civilian defense* has been used. As such headings with this subdivision are added to the catalog they would have to be added to the reference. Under these circumstances, a general reference is indicated, if the number of headings to be referred to is so large as to make it unlikely that many readers would want to consult the material under all of them. The general reference, added to the specific "see also" reference, reads: *also* [*i.e., see also*] *subdivision* Civilian defense *under names of countries, cities, etc., e. g.*, Gt. Brit.— Civilian defense.

---

[4] As an extreme case of the number of entries in the catalog intervening between *Civil defense* and *Civilian defense* may be cited the public catalog of the Library of Congress, where no less than 10,646 subject entries and references and 720 title entries occur in this space, including, by way of example, 3,100 entries under the heading *Civil law*, 4,500 under *Civil procedure*, and 2,000 under *Civil service*.

IV. Form of Main Heading

The form which a subject heading takes reflects the idiosyncrasies of the English language, the kind of public the catalog is to serve, and the size and character of the book collection. The number and kind of cross references and other integrating devices are in turn affected by the form of the subject headings. It is necessary, therefore, to consider the different forms of subject headings.

Noun. The simplest form of subject heading is, obviously, a single noun, unmodified and without a qualifying phrase to explain or limit it, such as *Botany*, covering a broad field of subject matter; *Syndicalism*, a more restricted term, yet covering a fairly wide range of subject matter; and *Gallows*, very near the limit of desirable specificity in a catalog. "See" references are indicated from synonymous terms and such variant spellings as would permit other headings to be filed alphabetically between the spelling adopted and the spelling from which the reference is made. If the synonyms (or headings other than synonyms in lieu of which the heading adopted is used) are in the form of adjectival or compound phrases, such "see" references should be made from inverted forms as would be required, say, in the case of adjectival or compound headings. (*Cf. infra* Adjectival Headings; Compound Headings.) Examples: *Ethics*, refer from *Deontology; Morality; Morals; Moral philosophy; Philosophy, Moral.*

Adjectival Headings. Frequently a subject can be best expressed by an adjectival phrase consisting of an adjective or an adjectival noun followed by the noun modified. There are several types of adjectival headings, and the kinds of references they require depend to a considerable extent upon the type. The modifier may be a common adjective (*Agricultural credit, Real property, Electric waves*), a proper adjective (*Pythagorean proposition, Brownian movements, Eustachian tube*), or, and particularly, an ethnic or geographic adjective (*Spanish literature, Australian ballot, Jewish question, Indian warfare*), or, occasionally, a common or proper noun in the possessive case (*Sailors' songs, King's peace, Machinists' tools, Farmers' institutes, Euclid's Elements*), or, finally, a common or proper noun used as an adjective, but without an adjectival ending (*Electron microscope, La Tène period*).

It is important to consider the distinctions between the several types of adjectival headings, since the kind of "see" references needed varies with the type of heading. In general, no reference need be made if the generic term, that is, the noun, serves merely as the vehicle for the modifier which gives meaning to the phrase. Conversely, a reference is needed if the adjective, or adjectival noun, serves primarily to modify or qualify. In the heading *Agricultural credit* the term

21

"agricultural" indicates the kind of credit, "credit" being used otherwise both as an independent heading and in such headings as *Insurance, Credit; Letters of credit; Credit guides.* A "see" reference from the inverted form *Credit, Agricultural* is, therefore, clearly in order. Because *Credit* is used independently and as the initial word in other headings, a "see also" reference from *Credit* to *Agricultural credit* should also be made. The basis for this is the fundamental rule that pertinent references should be made between headings if they will appear in the catalog at some remove from each other and should be omitted if they will be filed next to each other, or at any rate, so close that neither is likely to be overlooked by the reader.

Headings introduced by an ethnic or geographic adjective do not, as a rule, require a reference from the inverted form. Instead, a "see also" reference is made from the generic term if it is used independently, that is, without qualification. No reference, for example, is required from *Drama, German* to *German drama*, a general reference from *Drama* being adequate to indicate to the reader that the ethnic adjective precedes the noun. If a reference from the inverted form were to be made in such instances, there would be nests of such references under each noun used in headings of this type. In the case of *Drama*, for instance, specific "see" references would be needed in most library catalogs from the following inverted forms: *Drama, American; Drama, French; Drama, German; Drama, Italian; Drama, Russian; Drama, Spanish;* etc.

Inverted Adjectival Headings. When it is desired to bring the noun in an adjectival heading into prominence, either in order that it may appear in the catalog next to other headings beginning with that noun, or because the adjective is used simply to differentiate between several headings on the same subject, the inverted type of adjectival heading is used. A reference should be made from the uninverted form, *e. g., Art, Medieval,* refer from *Medieval art; Geography, Economic,* refer from *Economic geography.*

Phrase Headings. The phrase heading is formed of two nouns with or without modifiers, connected by a preposition or conjunction, and used to express an other than additive relationship, *e. g., Women as authors, Church work with youth, Electricity on ships, Photography of children, Radio in navigation.* Excluded from this category are compound headings in which the relationship of the nouns is additive (hence the conjunction "and" is used) and phrases in which the preposition "in" is used to introduce a geographic name and which are in reality a type of heading with geographical subdivision.[1] Phrase headings serve the following purposes: 1) to limit a concept, or render it more specific, when this cannot be accomplished by using a single word or a noun with modifiers; 2) to express a relationship between two concepts or things; and 3) to express a concept for which a phrase is commonly used. *Photography of children* is an example of a heading in

---

[1] Headings with geographic subdivisions are discussed below.

which a prepositional phrase is needed to render the subject more specific; it is photography limited to one kind of photographer's subject—children. *Women as authors* illustrates a heading which expresses a relationship, the relationship between authorship and the sex of the author. *Divine right of kings* is a heading of the type in which a concept can only be expressed by the whole commonly-used phrase.

Because phrase headings are so varied in form as compared with other types of headings, no general rule with regard to the references required can be applied to them as a group. However, insofar as such headings follow particular word patterns, rules applicable to each can be formulated.

For phrase headings which express a relationship (for example, those in which the conjunction "as" occurs) no "see" references are required, if the members of the phrase have no synonyms or if the synonyms of the first member have been used as references to it as an independent heading. The heading *Clergymen as authors* requires references from the following headings: *Priests as authors*, *Priests as writers*, *Ministers as authors*, *Ministers as writers*, and, if the number of headings beginning with the word "clergymen" is sufficient to warrant it, also from *Clergymen as writers*. If there are references in the catalog from *Priests* and *Ministers of the gospel*, the references above which begin with these words can be dispensed with. For all phrase headings, however, "see also" references should be made from the second element, if it is also used as an independent subject heading—in this case, *Authors*—or from the synonym of the second element, if the synonym is used as an independent heading. In those instances where a synonym of the phrase heading as a whole exists, a "see" reference should obviously be made from this synonym. This is more frequently true of those headings which are used to express a single concept that can only be expressed by a phrase. *Figures of speech*, for example, requires "see" references from *Tropes* and *Figure of speech*, and possibly one from *Speech, Figures of* (on the assumption that some users of the catalog would look under the inverted form), and a "see also" from *Rhetoric*.[2]

Frequently the phrase chosen as a heading and an adjectival form using the same terms have equal standing in current usage, in which case reference from the adjectival heading should be made rather than from the inverted phrase. Examples: *Stability of ships*, refer from *Ships' stability*; *Rotation of crops*, refer from *Crop rotation*; *Symbolism of numbers*, refer from *Number symbolism* and *Symbolic numbers*. If the generic term is used as a heading with subdivisions, a reference should also be made from it with the first noun of the phrase as subdivision, e. g., from *Ships—Stability*, *Crops—Rotation*, respectively.

Inverted Phrase Headings. Uninverted phrase headings are to be preferred, since they represent the normal order of words and it can be reasonably assumed that most readers would not look under the inverted form. However, phrase

---

[2] In the Library of Congress catalogs *Figures of speech* is used for works on English figures of speech as well as figures of speech in general, hence a "see" reference is made also from *English language—Figures of speech*.

headings in inverted form are used when the first element in effect qualifies the second and the second is used in the catalog as an independent heading. The inversion is then equivalent to subdivision, but is used in place of subdivision to preserve the integrity of the commonly used phrase. A "see" reference to the inverted heading is to be made from the uninverted form and from other synonymous phrases, *e. g.*, *Plants, Protection of*, refer from *Protection of plants; Debt, Imprisonment for*, refer from *Imprisonment for debt.*

Compound Headings. A compound heading is one made up of two or more coordinate elements joined by the conjunction "and." This form of heading serves, in the main, three purposes: 1) to express a relationship between two concepts or kinds of things; 2) to cover works on two subjects or topics, sometimes opposites, which are generally treated together, yet must be named in the heading in order to show its scope; and 3) to provide for instances in which the second noun serves to explain the first. *Literature and morals, Church and education, Libraries and schools* are examples of compound headings indicating a relationship. *Medical instruments and apparatus, Idols and images, Bolts and nuts* illustrate headings covering two subjects usually treated together or two aspects of the same subject, both of which must be used in the heading in order to show its scope. *Files and rasps* and *Indicators and test-papers* are headings in which one noun helps to define the other. Coupled with "rasps," "files" obviously means "a steel instrument with ridges or teeth upon its surface, used for abrading or smoothing metal surfaces." Used together, "test-papers" and "indicators" can refer only to chemical indicators which show the beginning or end of a chemical reaction. In some instances, *e. g.*, *Gums and resins* and *Weights and measures*, the compound heading provides for topics usually treated together, while its elements define each other.

When the compound heading expresses a relationship, a "see" reference is clearly indicated from the heading with the nouns transposed, *e. g.*, *Literature and morals*, refer from *Morals and literature*. References should also be made from other phrases which are used to express this relationship, such as those in which synonyms for either the first or the second or both nouns are used; for example, *Church and education* requires a "see" reference from *Education and church*, and also from *Religion and education* and *Education and religion; Bible and geology*, references from *Geology and Bible, Geology and religion*, and *Religion and geology.*

For the other types of the compound heading a "see" reference from the second noun is required, unless the latter is derived from the same root. In the latter case, such a reference would be needed only if, due to the presence of entries other than subject, the two nouns would not adjoin each other in the catalog. *Moors and heaths*, for example, requires a "see" reference from *Heaths; Heresies and heretics*, on the other hand, does not require a reference from *Heretics*, since it would probably follow the heading *Heresies and heretics* in the catalog without any other headings intervening.

Composite Forms. In phrase and compound headings, adjectives and prepositional phrases are used to modify the noun, forming adjectival compound and phrase headings, and even compound phrase headings. The variety of combinations possible in the form of such headings makes it undesirable to treat each combination separately. Furthermore, few generalizations can be made with respect to the references needed for each combination, because factors applying both to adjectival and to phrase and compound headings may enter into the question as to which references are needed for individual headings of this composite character. Suffice it to say that the same references are usually required as in each of the various types represented in a composite heading.

In instances where two adjectives are used to define a noun, a "see" reference should ordinarily be made from the noun modified singly by each adjective, *e. g.*, *Open and closed shop,* refer from *Open shop* and *Closed shop; College and school drama,* refer from *College drama* and from *School drama.*

Where a single adjective is used to modify two nouns, a "see" reference is indicated from the second noun modified by the adjective, unless the second noun is derived from the same root and they differ only in their endings. Examples: *Tobacco jars and boxes* and *Political crimes and offenses* would require "see" references from *Tobacco boxes* and *Political offenses,* respectively, while in the case of *Coal mines and mining* no reference is necessary from *Coal mining.*

In the case of two adjectives used to modify one noun, or of one adjective used to modify two nouns, a reference from the inverted forms, respectively, of each adjective with the noun they modify, or of each noun with the adjective modifying both, is indicated under the same circumstances as those under which such a reference would be appropriate for a simple adjectival heading.

References should not be made on this basis where the adjectival or phrase compound headings are not descriptive but representative in character, that is, where they express a single concept or idea which requires a phrase for its expression. To this category belong such headings as *Freedom of the seas, Spheres of influence, First aid in illness and injury, Employees' representation in management, Solemn League and Covenant.* The "see" references to be made for such headings depend solely upon their synonymy.

V. Subject Subdivision

A general exposition of all phases, or the major part, of a subject requires only a simple word or phrase heading. This is particularly the case where the number of works on the subject in the library's collections is relatively small: the reader should be able, in most cases, to select the title he wants from the several on the subject. Under certain conditions, however, a simple subject heading will not answer the purpose of the reader. If the number of works on the subject is large, or if the subject matter is presented from a special point of view or to serve a special purpose, or is limited with respect to the time or place covered or the type of facts presented, it becomes necessary to modify the heading by the use of the device called subdivision. This device may also be used for special reasons to introduce a branch of the subject or topic, although, as will be explained below, this is to be avoided.

Subdivision is distinguished from qualification in that it is ordinarily used not to limit the scope of the subject matter as such, but to provide for its arrangement in the catalog by the form which the subject matter of the book takes, or the limits of time and place set for the subject matter. In the catalogs of the Library of Congress it is identifiable by the use of the dash to separate the main element of the heading from the subdivision, as well as by the precedence, in the arrangement of the entries, of the subdivisions of a heading over that heading followed by a qualifying term.

Subdivision, as against the use of a word or phrase heading, is resorted to when no invariable, commonly used and accepted phrase is available with which to express the intended limitation of a subject. Thus, while *Geology* is the obvious heading for that subject, there is no set phrase for a dictionary or encyclopedia of geology under which most readers would inevitably look. However, aspects of a subject or topics comprehended within it are likely to be sought under names of their own, hence, as a rule, require entry under independent headings, rather than subdivisions under the broad subject. The contrary practice yields headings of the alphabetico-classed type, the advantages and disadvantages of which have been brought out earlier, in the discussion of the types of subject catalogs. Subdivision should as far as possible be limited to the form in which the subject matter is presented and the place and time to which it is limited.

Form Subdivision. Form subdivision may be defined as the extension of a subject heading based on the form or arrangement of the subject matter in the book. In other words, it represents what the book is, rather than what it is about, the subject matter being expressed by the main heading.

Let us take for example a group of works on agriculture which cover the whole range of the subject, or the greater part of it, or such a miscellany of topics in it that they cannot be assigned to a particular branch or aspect of it. Such a group would still embrace a variety of forms of presentation and arrangement which would make it necessary to break it up into smaller groups on that basis, as follows:

Agriculture—Abstracts.
 —Addresses, essays, lectures.

> For a miscellany of short contributions to the subject not systematically organized, or for brief, yet broad, addresses on agriculture containing little of the factual content of the subject.

 —Collected works.

> For collections of works covering all or most phases of the subject, whether works by a single personal author, or a series published by a society or institution.

 —Outlines, syllabi, etc.
 —Periodicals.
 —Yearbooks.

To this category of general works belong comprehensive works which present a particular approach, a particular type of data, a particular function or use, as expressed in the following form subdivisions:

Agriculture—Bibliography.
 —Congresses.

> For proceedings, that is, data presented at congresses of specialists.

 —Dictionaries.
 —Early works to 1800.

> To bring together works primarily of historical interest.

 —History.

> For the history of the progress of the art and science of agriculture

 —Juvenile literature.

> For works intended for juvenile readers.

 —Laboratory manuals.
 —Maps.
 —Pictorial works.
 —Quotations, maxims, etc.
 —Societies, etc.

> *cf.* Agriculture—Congresses *above.*

 —Statistics.
 —Study and teaching.

> For works on schools of agriculture and methods of teaching the subject.

 —Terminology.

> For discussions of the vocabulary of agriculture and lists of words not of the nature of dictionaries.

A comprehensive list of such form subdivisions as are generally applicable appears in an appendix to the text.

Local Subdivision. When the data of the subject treated are limited to a geographic or political area, the heading may be subdivided by the name of the place. This method of subdivision is variously called place, local, or geographic. It is applicable to such subjects as possess a geographic connotation. However, it should not be used where the geographic element is merely incidental, as in the citation of examples to illustrate the principles or facts treated. In a treatise on economics published in England, for example, economic principles and facts may be illustrated from English economic life, although the intent of the author in such a case would not be to describe English economic life.

Theoretically, any subject may be subdivided by place. However, scientific and technological topics which do not usually possess a local connotation do not require place subdivision. This is not the case with many broad subjects in the fields of science and technology, particularly the so-called earth sciences, and headings designating industries. Headings in the social sciences and law obviously lend themselves to subdivision by place. Nevertheless, where the topic is extremely specific and the literature meager, place subdivision can be dispensed with, since it would make the subject heading structure too elaborate for the user of the catalog. Whenever the amount and character of the material in the library warrants it, local subdivision may be applied to a heading previously unsubdivided.

Examples of broad headings in science and technology subdivided by place are *Agriculture, Geology, Television. Albumin, Electrons, Pipe flanges,* on the other hand, bear no relation to place and are not subdivided geographically. *Euthanasia, Marks of origin, Overtime,* originally unsubdivided by place, require subdivision because of the increase in the literature of these subjects.

Direct vs. Indirect Subdivision. There are two methods of geographic subdivision in use, the indirect and direct. Indirect subdivision interposes the name of the country or state between the subject and the place within that country or state to which the subject matter is limited.

> Agriculture—Mexico—Yucatan.
> Agriculture—Kansas—Haskell Co.

Headings for which direct subdivision is indicated are followed immediately by the name of the specific place, without the interposition of the name of the country or state, as follows:

> Art—Paris, *not* Art—France—Paris;
> Art—Toledo, Spain, *not* Art—Spain—Toledo;
> Employment agencies—Atlanta, *not* Employment agencies—
>   Georgia—Atlanta.

In general, headings in science and technology, especially broad headings, are subdivided indirectly, *e. g.*, *Agriculture, Meteorology, Mollusks, Gold mines and mining*. On the other hand, headings in law are almost invariably subdivided directly, *e. g.*, *Contracts, Railroad law, Habeas corpus*, and headings in the social sciences are generally so subdivided.

Indirect subdivision assumes that the interest and significance of certain subjects are inseparable from the larger area—the country or state—or that the study of subordinate geographic areas is best considered as contributing to the study of the larger area. This kind of reasoning is clearly justified in the indirect subdivision of *Reformation*, since the Reformation was a broad movement, which varied in its course and character from country to country, but the significance of which can hardly be considered local with reference to a particular region or city. Therefore,

> Reformation—Germany—Palatinate, *not* Reformation—Palatinate;
> Reformation—Switzerland—Geneva, *not* Reformation—Geneva.

Nevertheless, it would be difficult to demonstrate the validity of this kind of reasoning in regard to many of the headings which have in the practice of the Library of Congress been subdivided directly. Thus, *Coal* and *Coal mines and mining* are subdivided indirectly, while *Coal-miners* is subdivided directly, *Legislative bodies* indirectly, *Library legislation* directly.

Apart from the fact that there can be no consistency in determining which headings are to be subdivided indirectly and which directly, there is a practical difficulty involved in the use of indirect subdivision. It arises from the practice 1) of using names of certain geographic areas directly as subdivision, omitting the name of the country or state in which they are found,[1] and 2) of using names of cities following the name of the country rather than of the subordinate region, even when the latter requires direct subdivision under any circumstances. To illustrate,

> Geology—Germany—Bonn,

yet

> Geology—Prussia, *not* Geology—Germany—Prussia.

Indirect subdivision of *Geology* should presumably bring together all material on the geology of Germany, yet Prussia, which is a part of Germany, is always used as a subdivision directly without the interposition of *Germany*, while Bonn, the name of a city in Prussia, is used as a subdivision not under *Prussia*, but under *Germany*, for the reason that cities are identified in library catalogs by the addition of the name of the country (except for the most important or best known cities, whose names are used without qualification).

Whenever the name of a place is used in indirect subdivision, a reference

---

[1] A list of places (states, provinces, etc.) which are always used directly as subdivisions is given in Appendix E.

should be made from the subject followed by the name of the place without the interposition of the name of the country.

Geology—Bonn

see

Geology—Germany—Bonn

However, this would still fail to bring together under *Geology—Prussia* the material on the geology of all places in Prussia.[2]

There is good reason for using certain names of places directly following the subject, even when indirect subdivision is clearly indicated for it.   The following categories of places are always used as direct subdivisions: names of the States and territories of the United States and of other federal governments; the cities of Washington, D. C., and New York; historic regions, states, and principalities, including particularly those which have had an independent political existence and now form a part of more than one state; and ecclesiastical provinces which do not fall wholly within, or are not wholly identified with, one political jurisdiction.   In the case of states and provinces of a federal government, the use of indirect sub-division would concentrate an extremely large number of entries under one geographic subdivision.   This would be particularly true in the case of the States of the United States, *e. g.*, if *Agriculture—U. S.—Alabama,* [*Illinois, Nebraska, etc.,*] were used instead of *Agriculture—Alabama, Agriculture—Illinois, Agricul-ture—Nebraska*, etc.   Furthermore, the full list of the names of the states or prov-inces of any federal government can be readily ascertained if a user of the library were to ask for the material on the country including that on the individual states and provinces.

The regions, states, and provinces which had a separate existence from the existing states of which they are a part, or which are not wholly within the bound-aries of an existing state, must obviously be used as direct subdivision.   Any other use would be misleading and would fail to meet the needs of readers inter-ested in the particular area without reference to the larger country of which it is now a part.   As for the two cities, the amount of material in American libraries on New York, and at the Library of Congress on Washington, D. C., makes it desirable to make the approach to them as direct as possible.   By the same token, any library might make the subdivision direct for the most important city in the state or the one on which its collections contain an extraordinary amount of material.

Direct subdivision offers but one problem: how to bring to the reader the material on one state, province, or country, when it is scattered under names of cities, counties, lakes, river valleys, etc., within it.   The solution to this problem is that which the subject catalog affords in any subject field: if desired, references can be made from the subject heading subdivided by an inclusive area to all places within the area which have been used as subdivisions under that subject heading.

---

[2] In view of the above reasoning, practice in the Library of Congress has tended increasingly toward direct subdivision.

Furthermore, references can be made from more than one inclusive area to the same subdivision. For example, under indirect subdivision a work on the geology of Fort Lauderdale, Florida, is entered as follows:

Geology—Florida—Fort Lauderdale.

It is assumed that the reader who wants all the books in the library on the geology of the United States would seek it under the following subdivisions: *U. S.*, the names of all the States, *District of Columbia, Washington, D. C., New York (City)*— subdivision being direct to the States, the District of Columbia, and these two cities—and the names of rivers, valleys, mountain ranges, geographic regions, and the like. References are not ordinarily made by catalogers from *Geology—U. S.* to all of these other subdivisions. By the same token, a work on the geology of Fort Lauderdale could be found by the reader, if it were entered under the heading *Geology—Fort Lauderdale, Fla.*, and reference were made from *Geology—Florida* and from *Geology—Broward County* to this heading. The reader who desires all the material on the geology of Florida would then be certain to find *Geology—Fort Lauderdale, Fla.*

Because of the complications involved in the use of indirect place subdivision and the consequent likelihood of deviations and errors, there is a tendency to dispense with this method. It is continued only in types of headings in which its use has been consistent. For headings which obviously require subdivision by place but are not related to those which have previously been subdivided indirectly, direct subdivision is indicated.[3]

The basis for subdivision of some subjects *by* place and the use of other subjects as subdivisions *under* names of places is not likely to be clear to the reader. It is, therefore, necessary to provide references to subjects with local subdivisions from the names of the places used with the subjects as subdivisions. When, for example, the heading *Geology—Illinois* is used, a reference should be made from *Illinois—Geology*, since it is conceivable that the reader might turn to the name of the place, rather than the subject. Theoretically, such reference might be made in all cases where a given place is used as a subdivision under a subject. However, it is unlikely that a reader interested in a specific topic would use this approach. Therefore, reference from place subdivided by subject is ordinarily made only in the case of broad subjects and such others as clearly have a local connotation. Thus, a reference from *Japan—Geology* is obviously necessary, *Japan—Railroads* possibly so, but a reference from *Japan—Porcelain* would be of doubtful usefulness.

In the case of indirect subdivision, the references form a more elaborate

---

[3] *Subject Headings with Local Subdivision* (4th edition, 1925) shows a ratio between headings with indirect and headings with direct subdivision of approximately 2 to 1; in the 5th edition, 1935, the ratio is 17 to 16, representing an increase in headings with direct subdivision, as well as some changes from indirect to direct. In *Subject Headings . . . Supplement to the 5th edition, July 1947–December 1948* only about 8 percent of the headings for which local subdivision is indicated are to be subdivided indirectly.

pattern.   Reference should always be made from the subject with the specific place as subdivision to the form of heading actually used.

> Agriculture—Cork (County)
>> *see*
> Agriculture—Ireland—Cork (County)

If there are in the catalog subdivisions under the given subject for an intermediate jurisdiction of which the specific place is a part, the pattern of cross references is as illustrated by the following:

> Geology—England—Clapham (Surrey)
>> (the qualification "(Surrey)" being used to distinguish it from places of the same name in Bedfordshire, Sussex, Yorkshire, etc.)

> Clapham, England (Surrey)—Geology
>> *see*
> Geology—England—Clapham (Surrey)

> Geology—Surrey
>> *see*
> Geology—England—Surrey

> Geology—England—Surrey
>> *see also*
> Geology—England—Clapham (Surrey)

This pattern would apply, of course, whether or not the name of the intermediate jurisdiction is given following the specific place, as in this example.   Thus, references would have to be to *Geology—Germany—Berlin* from *Geology—Berlin* and *Geology—Prussia* (in the latter case a "see also" reference) even though "Berlin" is used as the name of the principal city in Germany without any qualification whatever.

Period, or Time, Subdivision.   The most obvious type of heading which requires subdivision by period is the heading for the history of a place or subject.   If the amount of material in the library on the history of a country, state or province, or city is small, there is little need for a period subdivision.   However, even a small American library is likely to have a considerable number of books on American history or the history of its own state, some of which would be limited to particular periods.   As a general rule, therefore, headings in the field of history should be subdivided by period.   The period subdivisions used should either correspond to generally recognized epochs in the history of the place or should represent spans of time frequently treated in books, whether they possess historic unity or not.   In many instances these two categories of time subdivision coincide; frequently, however, a sequence of years or events which may not prove epochal appears as the subject of relatively voluminous literary treatment, *e. g.*, the twentieth century, the Gay Nineties.

If the period is accorded a name, it should be included in the period subdivision. However, it is the terminal dates which clearly define the period and, even where the name of the period is used, the dates should follow. The date, furthermore, makes the sequence of periods in the catalog clear, while the name, if used alone, would make it difficult, sometimes perhaps impossible, for the reader to find.

> U. S.—History—Queen Anne's War, 1702–1713.
> U. S.—History—1815–1861.
> U. S.—History—20th century.

Because terminal dates are not always easy to establish, or because there is disagreement about them, or because certain periods and events are familiar to readers, they are sometimes omitted. This practice should, however, be avoided as far as possible.

> U. S.—History—Revolution.
> U. S.—History—Civil War.
> France—History—Revolution.

The only references needed are those from the name of the period or event, *e. g.*,

> Queen Anne's War, 1702–1713
> > *see*
> U. S.—History—Queen Anne's War, 1702–1713
>
> American Revolution
> > *see*
> U. S.—History—Revolution

The presence in the catalog of broad period subdivisions does not preclude the use of subdivisions covering events or lesser epochs falling within the broad period. Because the arrangement of headings with period subdivisions is chronological rather than alphabetical, the lesser periods will follow the greater without complication.

> Germany—History—1517–1648.
> Germany—History—1618–1648.
> Germany—History—18th century.
> Germany—History—1740–1806.

Wars in which two or more countries participated are entered under their own names with references from the names of the participants followed by the appropriate period of their history.

Franco-German War, 1870–1871.

France—History—Franco-German War, 1870–1871
see
Franco-German War, 1870–1871

Germany—History—Franco-German War, 1870–1871
see
Franco-German War, 1870–1871

Reference should be made from variant terms applied to the war, *e. g.*,

Franco-Prussian War, 1870–1871
see
Franco-German War, 1870–1871

By way of exception, wars, other than those of world-wide scope, in which the United States (or the American colonies) took part are entered under *United States*.

U. S.—History—King William's War, 1689–1697.
U. S.—History—Queen Anne's War, 1702–1713.
U. S.—History—Tripolitan War, 1801–1805.

Battles are entered not under the war heading, but under their own names, with "see also" references from the war headings, on the assumption that those who seek material on a particular battle would look for it under its name, rather than the war of which it was an incident.

Chronological or time subdivisions are also used under various subjects, when it is desired to segregate material covering a certain period or published before a certain date.

Aeronautics—Early works to 1900.
Apologetics—Middle Ages.
Apologetics—17th century.
Arithmetic—Before 1846.
Arithmetic—1846–1880.

Here, too, the dates should not be arbitrarily chosen. They should represent a turning point in the development of the literature of the subject. The end of a century is often deemed to be epochal and may be used as a time subdivision. However, the century would obviously vary with the subject: in education, 1800 may be a convenient or even significant date, whereas, in aeronautics, it would be of virtually no significance at all. Histories of the literature of a subject may be used to advantage in determining which dates are sufficiently significant for the purpose of time subdivision.

Subdivision by Topic. As stated earlier, the use of topics comprehended within a subject as subdivisions under it is to be avoided. It is contrary to the principle of specific entry, since it would, in practice, result in an alphabetico-classed catalog. Insofar as a division or phase of a subject, or a topic comprehended within it, may be clearly expressed by a word or a phrase heading, there is little warrant for its use as a subdivision of a broad heading. References from the broad heading will lead the reader to the specific headings subordinate to it. That subject catalogs, as a matter of fact, contain headings subdivided by topics is evidence of a lack of a clear understanding of the purpose of the alphabetical subject catalog and of the distinction between a specific heading of the direct type and an alphabetico-classed heading.

Many headings which appear to violate this rule in effect resemble alphabetico-classed headings in their outward form only. Actually they employ the form of subdivision by topic only where the broad subject forms part of the name of the topic and a convenient phrase form sanctioned by usage is lacking, or, for the purposes of the catalog, where it is desirable to conform to an existing pattern.

In the heading *Heart—Diseases*, for example, the alphabetico-classed form permits the grouping of entries for works on the diseases of the heart with works on abnormalities of the heart. If the same wording were used as a phrase—*Heart diseases*—entries under names of societies and institutions and under titles would separate in the catalog the entries for works on the heart in general, on abnormalities of the heart, and on the diseases of the heart.

"Research" is used as a subdivision under a variety of subjects, both broad and narrow, but only when the word cannot conveniently be used as part of a phrase heading, especially where there is no phrase clearly sanctioned by usage. Therefore,

> Agricultural research,
> Historical research,
> Psychical research,

but

> Insurance, Social—Research,

since *Social insurance research* would be separated completely from the heading *Insurance, Social*. Similarly,

> Social psychology—Research,

since "social psychology research" is not a commonly used term; "research in social psychology" is perhaps the usual way in which the concept is referred to, but to use even this phrase would separate the heading from *Social psychology*.

When this form of subdivision is used, reference from synonymous phrases of less common acceptance is made. The "see also" reference from *Research* will serve to guide those readers who seek material on research in all fields under this heading to the headings with the subdivision *Research*, as well as to the direct and inverted phrase headings, such as *Historical research* and *Research, Industrial*.

VI. Individual Names as Subject Headings

A critical, historical, or biographical account of an individual requires, with certain possible exceptions, a subject entry under his name. This applies to persons both real and imaginary, as well as to corporate bodies (government agencies, private associations and institutions), exploring expeditions, anonymous works of literature or art, ships, animals which are identified by name, structures (buildings, bridges, etc.), and any other individual entities bearing a proper name. Such entries make it possible for the reader to find all of the separately published and separately cataloged material on a particular person or thing without having to search under a broad class heading. For the benefit of those readers who might seek it under a broader heading, general or specific references should be made from the immediate topic or class within which the individuals are comprehended. The type of reference required depends on the category of the individual name.

Personal Names. The principal kinds of books about a person which require a subject entry under his name are biographies, characterizations, eulogies, criticisms, bibliographies, and literary works in which he figures. The form of name used as the subject heading should, in general, follow the *A. L. A. Cataloging Rules for Author and Title Entries*, which should govern in the matter of choice of form, where several are available, and of the references to be made. In a dictionary catalog, the same references will serve for the name, whether used in an author, secondary, or subject heading.

Where the literature about a person is voluminous, it is desirable, in order to make it easier for the reader to orient himself and to limit his search, to subdivide the name heading by the form of the material, such as *Anecdotes; Bibliography; Cartoons, satire, etc.; Portraits.* If it is desired to bring together in the catalog literary works of which the person is the subject or in which he largely figures, such subdivisions as *Drama, Fiction,* and *Poetry* are used. If the extent of the literature justifies, other subdivisions may be used, including such as will represent aspects and stages of his life.[1] Ordinarily the subdivision *Biography* or *Criticism and interpretation* need not be used, since for general biographical and critical material the name alone would suffice. However, if the amount and variety of the material makes it desirable or necessary, it is possible to use these subdivisions. To separate the different aspects and stages in the life history of

---

[1] *Cf.* special tables of subdivision for Shakespeare and Lincoln in Appendix G, which will serve as examples of the possibilities of subdivision under the name of an author and of an important figure in public life.

the subject, the subdivision *Biography* may be divided further, as in the case of Shakespeare.

> Shakespeare, William—Biography—Ancestry.
> > —Last years.
> > —London life.
> > —Marriage.
> > —Youth.

For the unique aspects of the life of such a subject, special subdivisions may be used.

> Shakespeare, William—Stage history—1625–1800.
> > —Forgeries—Collier.

> Lincoln, Abraham, pres. U. S.—Assassination.

> Napoléon I—Elba and the Hundred Days, 1814–1815—Drama.

The subdivisions used in the Library of Congress catalogs under Shakespeare and Dante may, in so far as they apply, be used as subdivisions under names of other authors where the literature is voluminous. The subdivisions which apply to Shakespeare or Dante uniquely will serve suggestively in developing unique subdivisions under names of other authors. The subdivisions under Washington, Lincoln, and Napoleon may be used similarly under names of other public figures, when the volume of the literature about them justifies subdivision in this degree.

Certain practices in the use of personal names as subject headings which have gradually evolved in the Library of Congress and have been adopted by other libraries require mention and consideration here. In the case of certain names of persons with a voluminous subject literature, dates of birth and other identifying phrases are omitted when the name is followed by subdivision. This is done for the sake of economy of space on the card and, to some extent, as a labor-saving device. Exception may be taken to this practice on the ground that the same name is used in both the full and the brief form, hence the filer must be able to identify the two forms and arrange the shorter following the longer form. It is conceivable that some readers might overlook the entries under the shorter form. (*Cf. Napoléon I, Emperor of the French, 1769–1821* and *Napoléon I.*) This objection may be met if desired by omitting the date and other qualifying terms in all headings, both author and subject, with or without subdivision, in the case of the most prominent person of the name. Such is, in fact, done for place names. *Berlin* is Berlin the capital of Germany and *Paris*, the capital of France, preceding, respectively, all other Berlins and Parises in the catalog whose names are qualified, hence follow the name of the major city in the arrangement of the entries in the catalog.

Another deviation from the rule of entry for personal names is the use of the unqualified name or even merely the surname of an author in a phrase heading.

> Shakespeare in fiction, drama, poetry, etc.

> Burns, Robert, in fiction, drama, poetry, etc.
> Goethe as theater director.

This practice arises in part out of a desire to avoid the ambiguity of such a heading as *Shakespeare, William—Poetry*, which might be construed to represent a volume of Shakespeare's poems, rather than, as is intended, either Shakespeare as the subject of one or more poems, or a critical work on Shakespeare's own poetry. Headings of the type of *Shakespeare in fiction, drama, poetry, etc.* are used for discussions of the treatment of an author and his works in literature. The form *Goethe as theater director* avoids subdivision by a phrase beginning with a conjunction, presumably because the reader is unlikely to look for such a heading as *Goethe, Johann Wolfgang von—As theater director* among other headings with noun subdivisions beginning with "a," such as *Anniversaries, etc.; Appreciation; Autographs*. The objection to the use of the brief form of the author's name in a phrase heading is that it separates some of the entries for works about the author from the bulk of them, allowing names of other persons with the same surname, and names of places and titles beginning with the same word to come between the two groups.

While it may be impossible to avoid recourse to such a device, care should be taken to make all the necessary references from the main group of subject entries under the name to these deviations. References may be prepared on the following pattern:

> Goethe, Johann Wolfgang von—Poetry.
>
>> For poems about Goethe and works on the treatment of Goethe and his literary productions in poetry, *see* Goethe in fiction, drama, poetry, etc.
>
> Goethe, Johann Wolfgang von—Theater director
>> *see*
> Goethe as theater director
>
> Goethe, Johann Wolfgang von—Stage history
>> *see also*
> Goethe as theater director

Generally speaking, where the pattern of subdivision and variant forms of headings is intricate, as in the case of voluminous subjects, it is desirable to insert at the head of the file an outline of the system of subdivisions and variant forms. The attention of the reader should be drawn to the outline by using, in a card catalog, a card of special color or dimensions which will give it prominence.

Autobiographies. It is a common practice to omit the subject entry under the name of the biographee for autobiographical works. This is done for the obvious reason of economy, the entry under the author's name doing service both as author and as subject entry. However, this practice is to be deplored on at least two counts. The autobiography is, of course, often one of the best sources of biographical information about the author. Where there are several biographical works by other authors, or several editions of the same work by any one author, the autobiography is likely to be overlooked. This is true of autobiographies of such men as Benjamin Franklin, Benvenuto Cellini, and John Stuart Mill.

Furthermore, an autobiography, or an excerpt from one, is frequently published as part of another work, such as a collection of several biographies or a historical or sociological work on the period in which the biographee lived. Many libraries make analytical subject entries for the contents of such works. This has the effect of introducing entries into the catalog under the name of the biographee for only a part or particular editions of his autobiography.

A solution to this problem which would still answer the requirement of economy is afforded by using a single subject entry for each autobiography and referring to all editions of it under the name of the author, *e. g.,*

> Franklin, Benjamin, 1706–1790.
> The autobiography.
>> For separately published editions and translations of this autobiography *see* entries under the name of the author.

Corporate Names. Names of corporate bodies, including associations and firms, governments and their agencies, public and private committees and commissions, present no special problems in the subject catalog. Accounts of their origin and development, analyses and discussion of the organization and function of corporate bodies require subject entries under their names. A corporate name used as subject heading should invariably conform to that used as author entry, that is, it should follow the rules of author entry as regards form and references. The identity of the corporate body must, however, be clear.

There are instances where a physical plant owned or managed by a corporate body is the subject of a book. Even though the physical plant, *e. g.,* railroad, factory, or park, does not itself have corporate existence in the sense that authorship can be ascribed to it, its name must be used as the subject heading. The name of the corporate body should be used for works about that body specifically, not for works which are limited to the physical plant.

> Union Pacific Railroad Company.
>> for works about the firm, its history, corporate structure, etc.,

but

> Union Pacific Railroad.
>> for the railroad itself;

New York (State) Commissioners of Fire Island State Park.

> for works on the history, organization, and activities of the Commissioners,

but

Fire Island State Park, N. Y.

> for works about the park itself.

However,

Meissen.   Staatliche Porzellanmanufaktur.

> for both the firm and the factory, since the name stands for both.

If the names are distinct and are not likely to stand in the catalog in immediate proximity to one another, they should be connected by means of "see also" references.

According to the *A. L. A. Cataloging Rules for Author and Title Entries*, many entries under the names of corporate bodies partake of the character of autobiographies in that they are accounts of the origin, development, structure, and function of the corporate body.   The reasoning used above with reference to subject entry under autobiographies is also pertinent here.   It is, however, unnecessary to make subject entry or reference in the case of corporate bodies, for the reason that most of such works are not identified by readers as autobiographies. They are more likely to look solely under the author entries for information about the corporate body.

The same reasoning should be applied to expositions, expeditions, conferences, and similar entities of limited duration, which, though organized, sponsored, or managed by another corporate body, have an existence of their own and may serve as subjects.   Subject entry should be made under their own names, chosen in accordance with the rules of author entry, and "see also" reference made from parent or sponsoring corporate body, *e. g., Challenger Expedition, 1872–1876*, with "see also" reference from **Gt. Brit.** *Challenger Office*.

Names of Mythological, Legendary, Biblical, and Imaginary Characters. Beings whose existence belongs in the realm of myth or pure literary invention may achieve identity to a point where books are written about them.   Names of such beings may be used as subject headings exactly as those of real persons.   The same rules apply with respect to the choice of form of name and references.   The best-known English form should be given preference and references made from other, including vernacular, forms.   There is little objection to the use of diacritical marks since they would most likely be required for lesser known names, interest in which is primarily on the part of scholars accustomed to transliterated forms and to diacriticals.   "See also" references should be made to the name from the heading for the mythology, cultus, and literary source (personal author, anonymous classic, and the like). Biblical personages should be treated similarly.

> Daphne (Nymph)
>> Refer from ("see also") *Mythology, Greek* and *Apollo.*
>
> Siegfried.
>> Refer from ("see also") *Mythology, Germanic; Legends, Germanic;* and *Nibelungenlied.*
>>
>> Refer to ("see also") *Nibelungenlied.*
>>
>> "See" references should be made from variant forms of Siegfried's name.
>
> Gideon, judge of Israel.
>> Refer from ("see also") *Bible. O. T.—Biography.*
>>
>> Refer from ("see") the English variant *Gedeon, judge of Israel.*

Proper Names of Other Kinds. In general, anything so individualized as to bear a proper name may serve as the subject of a book. Ships, whose names may, according to the *A. L. A. Cataloging Rules for Author and Title Entries,* be used as author entries for official logs, frequently have books written about them, in which case the same form of name should be used for subject as for author entry. References should be made from the broader heading for the type of ship or from the event or category of events in which the ship figured. Names of famous horses, buildings, individual monuments, etc., may similarly be used as subject headings. References should be made from the next broader category of heading within which the subject matter covered by the specific heading would fall.

> Titanic (Steamship)
>> Refer from ("see also") *Shipwrecks.*
>
> Deutschland (Submarine)
>> Refer from ("see also") *Submarine boats.*
>
> Man o' War (Race horse)
>> Refer from ("see also") *Horse-racing.*
>
> Angkor Vat (Temple)
>> Refer from ("see also") *Temples—Indochina* and *Indochina— Antiquities.*

Pisa. Campanile.

Refer from ("see also") *Towers* and *Architecture, Medieval.*

"See" references should be made from variant forms of the name, such as *Leaning Tower, Pisa; Pisa. Leaning Tower;* and *Campanile, Pisa.*

New York. Cleopatra's Needle.

Refer from ("see also") *New York (City)—Monuments* and *Obelisks.*

Refer from ("see") *Cleopatra's Needle, New York* and *New York. Egyptian Obelisk.*

Individual Works of Literature. Criticisms or commentaries on individual books—works of which a given book is the subject—require subject entry under the basic heading used to identify the book.

In the case of books by personal or corporate authors, the subject consists of the name of the author accompanied by the form of the title which is used as a filing title. The precise form of the author's name used in the author entry serves the purpose of the subject heading, with the exceptions brought out in the chapter on personal names. The form of the title to be used in the subject heading is obviously that used by the author of the work. In many instances, however, titles of the several editions of the work vary. In the case of literary classics, the work is commonly known and cited by a briefer title, in part because of variation in the form of the title as it appears on the title-pages of the several editions, and in part because the title is too long or involved to be used in referring to the book. Where a brief form is used as a filing title for keeping all editions of the book together, the same short form should be used in the subject heading for works about it. Thus the subject heading for Shakespeare's *Hamlet* will be

Shakespeare, William.
Hamlet.

or, for economy of space,

Shakespeare, William. Hamlet.

rather than

Shakespeare, William.
The tragicall historie of Hamlet, prince of Denmarke.

This will keep the subject entries next to the author and the added entries in which the author's name and title are used in the heading. The references from the variant forms of the title will direct the reader to all three groups of entries—author, added entry, and subject. Where a short form of the title is not used as a filing title, yet the titles of the several editions vary, the earliest form is to be used for the subject as for other entries. On the other hand, Milton's *Defense of the*

People of England, sometimes cited as *Milton against Salmasius* would appear as a subject in the following form:

> Milton, John.
> > Pro populo anglicano defensio.

or, in a popular library, perhaps,

> Milton, John.   A defence of the people of England.

Sacred Books and Anonymous Classics.   A criticism, commentary, or other work dealing with an anonymous classic requires a subject entry under the form of name adopted as the main entry heading for editions of the classic under the *A. L. A. Cataloging Rules for Author and Title Entries.*   When the subject of such a work is one of the parts of a composite anonymous classic, the form of heading prescribed for the name of the part should be used as subject heading.   It is doubtful, however, whether, in such instances, the extension of the heading *beyond* the name of the part is of much use to the reader.   It would result in scattering the subject entries for the given part among main and added entry headings which continue beyond the name of the part, specifying the language, date of publication, and the like.   For example, editions of the book of Isaiah in the Old Testament might justify such a main or added entry heading as **Bible.**   *O. T. Isaiah.   Eskimo.   1837.   Bohemian Brethren,* or **Bible.**   *O. T. Isaiah XV–LXVI.   English.   1914.*   It would be unwise, however, to scatter commentaries on these versions under the full form of the main entry heading.   The subject heading *Bible.   O. T.   Isaiah—Commentaries* would suffice.

Subject headings for the whole, or an individual book, of an anonymous classic may, if necessary, be subdivided by the form or aspect of the work.   This is particularly necessary under the heading for the Bible and its parts, since all libraries are likely to have a number of critical and exegetical works, concordances, and dictionaries.   As in the case of voluminous authors, special subdivisions are applicable to the Bible, which would be inappropriate for other works.   However, the subdivisions used in Bible subject headings should serve as a general pattern for other anonymous classics.

> Bible.   O. T.   Ezra,

but not

> Bible.   O. T.   Ezra.   Aramaic;

> Vedas.   Yajurveda,

but not

> Vedas.   Yajurveda.   English.   Selections;

> Bible—Commentaries;

> Bible.   O. T.—Concordances.

VII. Geographic Names as Subject Headings

Geographic names play a large part in the alphabetical subject catalog, both because geographic areas as such are of interest to library users and because many narrow topics as well as broad subjects are treated in the catalog with reference to place. A reader may wish to find a book on Iceland or the Ural Mountains on the one hand, or on farm tenancy in Illinois on the other. While many geographic names are used in a dictionary catalog both as author and secondary headings, as well as subject headings, there are certain categories which are used only as subject headings. Moreover, there are differences in the use of geographic names as subject headings and as author headings. Both these considerations make it necessary to state the rules.

Usage and Consistency. Generally speaking, the same principles apply to geographic headings as to other subject headings. The aim is to select, as far as possible, those forms of geographic names with which most readers are likely to be familiar, hence the ones to which they will resort, and to refer from forms less well known and less frequently used. Once the choice has been made, the form adopted should be used consistently under all circumstances in order to obviate excessive resorting to references on the part of the reader. This principle of common usage has at least one important implication for the procedure to be followed in making a choice. No single authority can be admitted to govern the choice, unless that authority itself follows the principle of usage. The reader's interest transcends the authority of an official body having responsibility for selecting geographic names for official use. However, it should be noted that the Library of Congress, being an agency of the Federal Government, considers itself required by law to follow, currently and in the future, names as established by the United States Board on Geographic Names.

Whereas in the case of other types of headings there is sometimes a divergence in the name form used by different classes of readers (juvenile, lay, specialist), the use of a geographic name is but rarely restricted to a particular class. Usage can, therefore, be determined without reference to the kind of public for which the book is written or to the cultural level of the reader. Usage should be determined by consulting current gazetteers and other geographical works of reference and by checking these against current publications in geography and in related fields of knowledge. The recent use of a particular form of name, provided it is not an isolated case, would make it preferable to a more common form which evidence shows to be obsolescent.

Language of Headings. The language of the heading is fundamentally an aspect of usage and should respond to it. Of the several forms of a place name found in works of reference or monographs, that one is to be preferred which is found in English-language works, representing, therefore, the usage in English-speaking countries. Names of major or widely-known geographic and political areas usually have forms in English-speaking countries which vary from those used in foreign countries. This is particularly true of natural geographic features such as mountain ranges, seas and lakes, gulfs and bays, and rivers. It is also true of continents, countries, extinct historic and political divisions, and world-known cities. Conversely, smaller, remote, or little-known geographic entities are likely to possess names only in the vernacular, or, to lack English forms. No choice remains in this case but to use the vernacular form and, in the instance where the vernacular employs a non-Roman alphabet, the transliterated form which is most often found in English-language publications.

The following examples illustrate the use of both English and vernacular forms on the principle stated above:

> South America, *not* Sudamérica, *nor* América del Sur;
> Black Forest, *not* Schwarzwald;

yet

> Riesengebirge, *rather than* Giant Mountains.
>
> > It is interesting to note that in Italian usage the Italian form is preferred (Monti dei Giganti), while in French usage the German form is almost invariably employed rather than the French (Monts des Géants).

> Constance, Lake of, *not* Bodensee;
> Austria, *not* Oesterreich;
> Brittany, *not* Bretagne;
> Danube River, *not* the German *Donau*, the Bulgarian and Serbo-Croatian *Dunav*, the Czech *Dunaj*, the Hungarian *Duna*, or the Rumanian *Dunarea*;
> Vienna, *not* Wien;

on the other hand,

> Chelyabinsk, Russia;
> Tientsin.

Geographical Names in the Dictionary Catalog. Geographical names are used as author or secondary entries as frequently as they are used in subject headings. Official publications of political jurisdictions, such as countries, states, provinces, counties, districts, towns, and villages, are entered under their names as the whole or the initial element of the heading.[1] Obviously, all such names may be used as

---

[1] Publications of agencies of the jurisdiction are usually entered under the name of the jurisdiction followed by the name of the agency. Laws, ordinances, constitutions, charters, and treaties are usually entered under the name of the agency followed by an appropriate subdivision (*Laws, statutes, etc.; Ordinances, etc.; Constitution; Charters; Treaties, etc.*)

subject headings in much the same way as names of natural features on the earth's surface: a book may deal with agriculture in Russia or with agriculture in the valley of the Danube River, with the history of Chicago or the history of the Scandinavian Peninsula. As a rule, the form of name used in a subject heading should be the same as that chosen as an author heading. It is of some importance that the books about a country should be listed in the dictionary catalog in the closest possible proximity to the books of which that country is deemed by the rules to be the author. As a corollary, in choosing the form of name, account should be taken of its dual use as author and subject heading.

Nevertheless, there are instances where deviations from this rule are necessary, if not indeed unavoidable. This stems from the fact that the choice of name for a political jurisdiction must sometimes take into consideration its official name. The publications of Ireland under the present constitution are thus distinguished from those published under the authority of the Irish Free State, of Northern Ireland, and of Ireland under the British Crown by entering them under **Ireland (Eire)**, **Irish Free State**, **Northern Ireland**, and simply **Ireland**. Such distinctions are unnecessary and undesirable in subject headings relating to Ireland, insofar as they relate to the whole of Ireland or to such a major part of it as cannot be identified by a generally accepted name. Books about Ireland do not necessarily limit themselves to the periods covered by the constitutional changes implied by the various forms of names used as author headings. Excepting *Northern Ireland*, which represents a separate area that is geographically and politically identifiable, *Ireland* as subject heading refers to the area as a whole. Periods in the development of various aspects of Irish life may or may not correspond to the constitutional changes, hence are provided for by the device of period subdivision. Similarly, the Hawaiian Islands as author are represented in the catalog under **Hawaiian Islands** for the period prior to their incorporation in the territory of the United States and under **Hawaii (Ter.)** for the period following, whereas *Hawaiian Islands* suffices as a subject heading for both. In general, then, subject headings follow author headings in the form of geographical names where the names represent territorial differences and convey these differences to the public mind.

In those instances where two name forms are available, one of which has a political and the other a purely geographical connotation, the latter is to be preferred. It stands to reason that the purely geographical name will outlive the political one, since political frontiers and allegiances are in no way as permanent as the more natural boundaries which represent topographic, historic, or ethnographic units. It follows that *Yugoslavia*, for example, is preferable to *Kingdom of Serbs, Croats, and Slovenes* or *Serb-Croat-Slovene Kingdom*, and *Argentina* is to be preferred to *Argentine Republic*.[2] A further reason for preferring geographical to political names is that the latter not infrequently date the heading and render inappropriate its use with certain subdivisions: *Czechoslovak Republic—Antiq-*

---

[2] *Argentine Republic* and *Czechoslovak Republic* are the forms used in the catalogs of the Library of Congress.

uities is obviously a less accurate heading than would be *Czechoslovakia—Antiquities*. The incongruity of using a late or modern form of name in headings which relate to an existence under an earlier name is not as serious in the case of cities and towns as in the case of countries, since the name of a city or town is not, generally speaking, political, that is, it does not necessarily imply a change in jurisdiction or allegiance.

Forms of Headings. Place names beginning with an article are entered in the catalog under the article, except in the case of those generally used in English without the article. In either case a "see" reference should be made from the form rejected to the one adopted.

> La Rochelle, France.
>> Refer from *Rochelle, La, France*.

> La Paz, Bolivia.
>> Refer from *Paz, La, Bolivia*.

> Oporto, Portugal.

> Giza.
>> Refer from *El Gizeh* and other variant transliterated forms found in English (*El Geezeh, Ghizeh, Gizeh*).

Names of watering places in Germany and Austria beginning with the word "Bad" are entered under the name following "Bad" with reference from the name beginning with "Bad" and the inverted form.

> Eilsen, Ger.
>> Refer from *Bad-Eilsen, Ger.* and *Eilsen, Bad-*.

> Nauheim, Ger.
>> Refer from *Bad-Nauheim, Ger.* and *Nauheim, Bad-*.

Names of political divisions should be given as they appear officially, without inversion. Names of natural features which consist of a generic and specific term often require inversion to allow the specific term to appear as the entry word.

> Azov, Sea of.
> Dover, Strait of.

However, when the generic term is in a foreign language and has lost its generic significance for the English-speaking public, the heading should not be inverted.

> Ben Nevis. ("Ben" presumably="mountain")
> Mont Blanc. (rather than "Blanc, Mont")

The general principle followed here is that, once the generic term has come to be a part of the proper name of the place, it may properly serve as the entry word.

Diacritical marks in foreign geographical names are often dropped when the names are taken into English usage. However, where no English form of a name is available, the diacritical marks of the vernacular form should be retained. Thus, *Rio Grande* for the river which separates the United States and Mexico is written without the accent, while *Río Cuarto, Cuba*, retains the accent. In general, diacritical marks should be used where usage justifies them, especially since they sometimes affect the filing of the entries in the catalog, as in the case of the umlaut.

Transliteration of geographical names from a vernacular in a non-Latin alphabet should be resorted to only for names which occur rarely in English-language publications and for which, consequently, no accepted English form exists. Neither should consistency be sought in the transliteration of names emanating from any one vernacular, if English-language forms do exist for names from that vernacular. The important thing to bear in mind is that English usage justifies each name.

> Gorki, Russia, which, if transliterated according to the system used by the Library of Congress and the *A. L. A. Cataloging Rules for Author and Title Entries*, would be Gor′kiĭ.

> Grozny, Russia, for which the usual library transliteration would be Groznyĭ.

> Ryazan, Russia, for which the usual library transliteration would be Rîāzan′.

Qualified Headings: Generic Qualifiers. Names of natural geographic features generally consist of a specific and a generic term, *e. g., Volga River, English Channel, Rocky Mountains.* In most instances, especially in the case of well-known names, there is an accepted English form of the name, with the generic term, obviously, in English. The English form is to be preferred on the same grounds as for any other type of subject heading. When the generic term precedes, the heading should be used in its inverted form, the specific term being used as the entry word (*Dover, Strait of; Mexico, Gulf of*). References should be made from other English forms and from vernacular forms which occur in English-language publications. As a rule, no references are required from vernacular and other foreign language forms, the assumption being that the English-speaking reader who seeks information about a given place will know the English rather than some foreign-language form of the name. If, however, the geographic headings are assumed to serve the added purpose of a secondary approach to particular books and if foreign-language books are included in the catalog, there is reason for making references from the forms used in such foreign-language books or elsewhere in the languages of these books.

For the benefit of the reader who will seek the geographic name under the generic term, a general reference should be made. If the generic term is itself used as a heading (whether in the singular or the plural), the general reference will take the following form:

> Lakes.
>> For works on a particular lake, *see also* its specific name,
>> *e. g.*, Great Salt Lake; Bizerta, Lake of.

If the generic term is not used as a heading, a general reference should be made from it in the following form:

> Gulf of . . .
>> For works on a particular gulf, *see* the specific term in its
>> name, *e. g.*, Mexico, Gulf of; Aegina, Gulf of.

Whether the prepositional form is used or simply the generic term followed by the specific depends solely on usage. In the name given here, "Lake of Bizerta" rather than "Lake Bizerta" or "Bizerta Lake" is the accepted form.

As a rule, the generic term is in English even when the specific term is in the vernacular. There are instances, however, when the use of both terms in the vernacular is justified by American practice. Thus,

> Rio Grande (for the North American river),

but

> Rio Grande Valley;

> Río de la Plata (formerly the River Plate, its common name in English-speaking countries),

yet

> Verde River, Ariz., *rather than* Rio Verde, Ariz.

There are many examples of the use, due to an inadequate knowledge of the vernacular geographic vocabulary, of English generic terms coupled with the corresponding vernacular term.

> Tian Shan Mountains ("Shan"="mountains" in Chinese)[3]
> Faroe Islands (the "oe" itself meaning "island")
> Hwang-ho River ("ho"="river" in North Chinese)
> Sierra Nevada Mountains ("sierra" meaning "mountain ridge")
> *Cf.* Blue Ridge Mountains.

Although usage may justify such forms, they should be avoided wherever possible. The cataloger must, however, understand the etymology of foreign geographic names to be able to tell whether or not the generic term is incorporated in them.

---

[3] Library of Congress catalogs use *Thian Shan Mountains.*

Qualified Headings: Geographic Qualifiers. Names of places require as qualifier the name of the major, or larger, geographic or political area of which they are a part or in which they are situated, when the name of the place alone is not sufficient to identify it clearly in the mind of the user of the catalog. Particularly is this true in the case of places little known in the English-speaking world. A geographic qualifier is, of course, inevitable when there are two or more places bearing the same name.

Names of cities and lesser inhabited places require the name of the country or its usual abbreviation as a qualifier. Names of cities in the United States and Canada, by way of exception, are followed by the name or the usual abbreviation of the name of the state or province.[4]

> Beatrice, Neb.
> Victoria, B. C.
> Saint-Dizier, France.
> Dundee, Scot.
> Smolensk, Russia.

The largest and best known city of its name, however, is entered without qualification on the obvious assumption that most readers will seek information about the largest and best known, rather than any other of the same name. Using the name without qualification places it in the catalog ahead of other cities of the same name and thus brings it to the attention of the reader ahead of the others. Apart from this exception, a geographic qualifier is indicated in all instances where two or more places have the same name.

> Athens [for Athens in Greece],

but

> Athens, Ga.,
> Athens, Ohio;

> London [for London in England],

but

> London, Ont.

Names of counties in the United States and Canada are followed by the name of the state or province, elsewhere by the name of the country.

> Charlotte Co., N. B.,
> Durham Co., Ont.,
> East Feliciana Parish, La.,
>   (The parish in Louisiana corresponds to the county in other states.)
> Washington Co., Ohio,

but

> Limerick, Ire. (County)

---

[4]*A. L. A. Cataloging Rules for Author and Title Entries* (2d ed.; Chicago: American Library Association, 1949), pp. 236–37.

Where two or more places of the same name exist in the same country, state, province, or other similar jurisdiction, the name is further qualified by giving the name of a lesser distinguishing jurisdiction in curves.

> Washington, Ohio (Fayette Co.)
> Washington, Ohio (Guernsey Co.)
>
> Bradford, Eng. (Devonshire)
> Bradford, Eng. (Northumberland: Berwick-upon-Tweed Div.)
> Bradford, Eng. (Northumberland: Wansbeck Div.)
>
> Templemore, Ire. (Co. Mayo)
> Templemore, Ire. (Co. Tipperary)
>
> Athies, France (Aisne)
> Athies, France (Pas-de-Calais)

Since political change often brings with it, in addition to the retracing of political boundaries and the creation of new political entities, changes in the geographical names of the places involved, it is the part both of economy and good sense to avoid the use of geographical names which are subject to change. This is not often possible, since the names should correspond to usage, and usage is likely to respond to these changes. However, in the use of qualifying terms it is sometimes possible to choose one which is likely not to be affected by such changes. As a general rule, when the choice exists, the qualifying term should be a historic or a non-political one. Names of natural geographic features and names of regions which have lost their political significance belong to that category. Specifically, Asia Minor, Mongolia, Arabia, Sicily, are preferable to Turkey, Mongolian People's Republic, Hejaz, Italy, in qualifying names of inhabited places in these areas. This is particularly applicable with reference to large islands and to island groups.

> Bastia, Corsica, *rather than* Bastia, France.
> Syracuse, Sicily, *rather than* Syracuse, Italy.

Qualified Headings: Political, etc., Qualifiers. Similarly, when the same name is used for different political and ecclesiastical jurisdictions in the same country or state, a qualification, in parentheses, should follow the name.

> New York (Archdiocese)
> New York (City)
> New York (Colony)
> New York (County)
> New York (State)

Mexico.
    [the country]
Mexico (Archdiocese)
Mexico (City)
Mexico (Ecclesiastical Province)
Mexico (Empire, 1821–1823)
Mexico (Federal District)
Mexico (State)
Mexico (Viceroyalty)

The place or jurisdiction of first importance, or the one to which the name most commonly refers, requires no qualification. The qualifying term should be in English, if possible. Only when no clearly equivalent term exists in English should the vernacular be used; the legal or official term is then inevitable.

Diepholz (Grafschaft)
Göttingen (Fürstentum)
Kassel (Regierungsbezirk)

Geographic Names of the Ancient World. Geographical names of the ancient world, particularly those in ancient Greek and Roman culture areas, present a special problem. A given settlement may no longer be in existence, or may have persisted through the ages under a succession of names, or may have been displaced by later ones which cannot be considered as stages in the continuity of existence of the ancient site.

If the settlement is no longer in existence, its ancient name best known in the English-speaking world is to be adopted. However, in the case of Greek place names, the Latin form of name is to be preferred.[5] References should be made from the transliterated Greek form, as well as from variant forms which would not be filed contiguously to the chosen heading. For Biblical place names, the form found in the Authorized version is to be preferred. References should be made from forms used in other versions, as, for example, the Douay version.

In the case of places in the ancient world whose identity has survived to the present, the modern form of name should be used and references made from the classical and other variant forms.

Kea (Island), Greece,[6] *rather than* Ceōs or Keōs.
Agrigento (City), *rather than* Agrigentum.

However, if the ancient name represents a distinct epoch or the later name belongs to a different culture, both names may be used and "see also" references made to connect them. Thus, for example, both *Istanbul* (formerly *Constantinople*)

---

[5] By analogy with *A. L. A. Cataloging Rules for Author and Title Entries*, rule 58, p. 109.

[6] In Library of Congress catalogs the form used is *Kea (Keōs), Island, Greece*.

and *Byzantium,* or *Erech, Babylonia* and *Warka, Mesopotamia* have a place in
the catalog. Scope notes placed in the catalog where they are least likely to be
overlooked by the reader (on guide card preceding entries under the name) are
useful in shortening the reader's search.

The subdivision *Antiquities* may be dispensed with in case the place is known
only through archeological excavation or where our knowledge of it is limited to
its antiquarian remains.

> Erech, Babylonia.
> Dura, Syria.
> Megiddo.

Changes in Geographical Names. As is the case with other kinds of terms
used as subject headings, geographical names are displaced when they have
dropped out of common use. However, there is the added factor of political
changes to be taken into account. Whether they alter boundaries or not, such
changes bring forth new, officially authorized or preferred, place names. Thus,
the Bolshevik revolution brought about changes in the names of many cities of
Russia: Nizhni Novgorod to Gorki[7]; Tsaritsyn to Stalingrad; Petrograd to Leningrad (Petrograd itself being a change from St. Petersburg, which in 1914 appeared
too German for the capital of a state at war with Germany). As long as Lorraine
was a part of France, Thionville seemed adequate; in 1871, however, when
Lorraine and Alsace were joined to form a German province, Thionville became
Diedenhofen; in 1918 it resumed its French name; while under German occupation during World War II it undoubtedly was Diedenhofen again. The reading
public, which becomes familiar with each new name through current newspapers,
magazines, and books, will inevitably look for material on the place which is
the focus of contemporary interest under its latest widely-known name. Under
these circumstances the cataloger must make the necessary changes in the headings
in which the older name occurs and refer from the older to the later form of name.
If the older material is likely to be sought by readers but rarely, it may be left
under the old name and "see also" references made between the old and the
new accompanied by an explanation of the basis for the separation of the
material.

It should be borne in mind, however, that the change applies not only to
headings and subject references in which the name of the place is the entry word,
for example, *Leningrad—Statistics,* and to institutions entered under the name of
the place, such as *Leningrad. Publichnaia biblioteka* and *Leningrad. Tekhnolo-
gicheskiĭ institut,* but also to subject headings for which the name of the place
is a subdivision, as in the case of *Housing—Leningrad* and *Criminal statistics—
Russia—Leningrad,* and names of societies, firms, and the like, which are followed
by their location, for example, *Obshchestvo sotsiologii i teorii iskusstv, Leningrad.*
In many catalogs the official records of headings, including the record of place

---

[7] In the usual library transliteration: Nizhniĭ-Novgorod, Gor'kiĭ.

names used, are defective, to say the least. In the first place, libraries do not regularly and uniformly insert in their catalogs references from place subdivided by subject; neither do they ordinarily prepare subject authority cards for each subdivision of a heading in order that references of this kind might be traced. It is obvious, therefore, that a change in the form of name of one geographic entity may have many ramifications and may call for a considerable measure of perspicacity, if not clairvoyance, on the part of the cataloger. Where authority cards are available, as they but rarely are, for each geographic subdivision of a given subject heading, or where reference is invariably made from the name of the place subdivided by each subject under which it has been used to each such subject heading with the name of the place as subdivision, the change may be carried to completion with the assurance that no loose ends remain in the catalog. Where such authority cards are not available, the cataloger cannot be certain of finding and correcting changes in geographic names where these names are used as subdivisions. Under these circumstances, there is the likelihood that variant forms of the same name or various names of the same place will remain scattered through the catalog as subdivisions under names of subjects. Thus, the keeping of an authority file of subject headings in which every individual geographic subdivision is recorded under every subject heading used is the only practical way to avoid such a condition and to insure thoroughgoing changes, when changes become necessary.

Use of Sources of Information. Just as for subject headings in general, no single authority should be used in the choice of geographic names for the catalog by libraries not required by law to do so. This applies even to lists sanctioned by an official body, such as the United States Board on Geographic Names or the Permanent Committee on Geographical Names for British Official Use. Official bodies are sometimes guided by special considerations not fully applicable to the problem of the catalog, where usage is the prime consideration.

Insofar as periodical literature and current books in English show, whether by direct examination or by reference to indexes and bibliographies, a common preference for a particular form of name, the cataloger's choice is obvious. When it comes to the form of the name for a little-known place, or the choice of one from several equally common forms, the guiding hand of authority becomes useful, even indispensable. Such sources of information as official lists of geographic names, atlases, gazetteers, encyclopedias, guide-books, and books of travel and history should be resorted to. Where these sources are in English, preferably of American authorship, and of relatively recent date, and where the source has in addition the authority of an official body, the cataloger may accept the form upon which there is substantial agreement, provided there is no question in regard to the identity of the place to which any variant forms apply. In making the choice, the elements of agreement, recency, and authority must be weighed, as in all other aspects of cataloging which depend upon such sources of information. Reliance upon authority is inevitable where usage cannot be determined otherwise.

English-language authorities have a prior claim over foreign-language sources of information, regardless of the fact that the places to be named are outside the limits of an English-speaking country, since forms of names current in English-speaking countries serve primarily an English-speaking public. However, when English sources fail, the next choice is a vernacular source and, in the case of countries where the alphabet used is non-Roman, a transliterated form is proper. Transliterated forms based on the English pronunciation of the letters of the alphabet are to be preferred to those based on foreign pronunciations (for example, *Surabaya*, rather than *Soerabaja*). By the same token, forms found in non-English reference works should be accepted readily if they refer to places in the country of the reference work. Caution must be exercised in the case of Russian place names found in French, German, Italian, etc., reference works. The name of Nezhin, a city in South Russia (the Ukraine), as transliterated from the Russian in accordance with the transliteration table in the *A. L. A. Cataloging Rules for Author and Title Entries* (new orthography transliterated: Nezhin; old orthography: Ni͡ezhin), is listed in the *Times Gazetteer* as Nyezhin, in the *Nouveau Larousse Illustré* as Niéjin, in the *Grosse Brockhaus* as Neschin, and in the *Nomenclature Officielle des Bureaux Télégraphiques* of the International Telegraph Bureau as Nejin. In such instances, as in the case of disagreement among English-language authorities, that form which corresponds to or closely approximates the transliterated one (if possible, without diacritical marks) should be preferred.

VIII. Duplicate Entry

The term "duplicate entry" is used in at least two senses. In the *A. L. A. Glossary of Library Terms* [1] it is defined (under "Double entry") as entry "under two subject headings, one for subject and one for place, for subjects of local interest and for scientific subjects relating to a particular locality, *e. g., Birds—Ohio* and *Ohio—Birds.*" This use of double entry has virtually disappeared from American dictionary catalogs. Carried out consistently it would nearly double the bulk of the subject catalog. In place of this type of double entry, catalogers enter either under place with subdivision by form, place, or aspect of the subject, or under subject with place subdivision, and make a reference from the reverse of the heading. The reason for the choice between entry under place with subdivision and under subject with place subdivision is discussed earlier in this guide.

Current use of double entry is limited to headings which express a mutual opposition of two interests or points of view, *e. g., U. S.—Foreign relations—France* and *France—Foreign relations—U. S.* If all material were to be placed under one heading and a reference were made from the other, it would bring together all material serving one interest, but not the other equally important interest. In any case, it would be necessary to establish a policy governing the choice. In the above instance, if the policy were in favor of entry under the country whose name would come first alphabetically, all material on French foreign relations would be brought together under *France—Foreign relations* and its subdivisions by the other countries, and either "see" references would be necessary from the other country with the subdivision *Foreign relations—France* or a general "see also" reference from *France—Foreign relations.* In any case, it would accomplish for countries with names in the early part of the alphabet a concentration of material which would be denied for countries with names in the latter part of the alphabet. Furthermore, it would require the reader to seek material on the foreign relations of some countries not only under their names under which general works on their foreign relations would appear, but also under the names of other countries which precede them in the alphabet. Conceivably an exception could be made for the United States; the problem would, however, remain unchanged for other countries.

The headings for which duplicate entry can be justified on the grounds that

---

[1] *A. L. A. Glossary of Library Terms* . . . prepared . . . by Elizabeth H. Thompson. (Chicago: American Library Association, 1943), p. 49.

it meets the equal needs of two groups of readers fall in the main into the following patterns:

1) 1. U. S.—Foreign relations—France.

     2. France—Foreign relations—U. S.

        This pattern can obviously be used for the diplomatic relations between any two countries; for the diplomatic relations between the Catholic Church (*i. e.*, through papal legates) and a country, the following variant is used:

        1. Italy—Foreign relations—Catholic Church.

        2. Catholic Church—Relations (diplomatic) with Italy.

2) 1. Literature, Comparative—English and German.
     2. Literature, Comparative—German and English.

3) 1. English literature—Translations from Chinese.
     2. Chinese literature—Translations into English.

4) 1. Irish literature (English)
     2. English literature—Irish authors.

        This serves the purpose of bringing together collections of literary works, or historical and critical material about them, on the basis of the language in which they were originally written, as well as of the ethnic group to which the author belongs or the country of his origin. This method has been used for the different literary forms in the various literatures and for newspapers and periodicals the language of which is different in name from the ethnic group they serve or is one of several languages spoken in the country.

        However, it is doubtful whether the need to bring together the work of an ethnic group writing in an adopted language is great enough to warrant duplicate entry. This interest can be satisfied by means of references from the headings based on the name of the ethnic group to the headings based on the language according to the following pattern:

        Irish poetry (English)
          see
        English poetry—Irish authors

        By this means the contributions of Irish authors to English literature can be traced to the various headings with the subdivision *Irish authors.*[2]

---

[2] The Library of Congress has adopted this device for those literature headings for which the method of duplicate entry has not been previously used.

In the case of newspapers, the form of the duplicate heading may vary as circumstances require.

    1. Swiss newspapers (German)
    2. German newspapers—Switzerland.

        For newspapers in the German language published in Switzerland.

    1. Irish periodicals (English)
    2. English periodicals—Irish.

        For periodicals in the English language published in Ireland.

        [Exception: For periodicals in other than the English language which are published in the United States, the pattern used is *Swedish-American periodicals* with a "see" reference from *American periodicals, Swedish* and a "see also" reference from *Swedish periodicals*.]

5) 1. Students' songs, American.
     2. Harvard University—Songs and music.

        This duplicate entry is necessary for the reason that collections of student songs issued by a particular college or university are usually general in scope, but include, in particular, songs in honor of the college or university or about it.

There is another type of duplicate entry, which does not fall into any of the above patterns but which is frequently and consistently used. When a heading for which local subdivision is not provided must be used for a topic which is treated definitely with reference to a place, a duplicate entry is made under the next broader heading which admits of local subdivision. This is most often the case of works which deal with the occurrence in a given place of a genus or species of the plant or animal worlds. A work on gnatcatchers of California would thus require entry under

    1. Gnatcatchers.
    2. Birds—California.

and a work on the grasses of the genus *Poa* in Scandinavia under

    1. Poa.
    2. Grasses—Scandinavia.

The reasoning which underlies duplicate entry of this type is that the interest is primarily in the kind of plant or animal, not in the place in which it is found, that the subject is usually treated without reference to place, and that the geographic interest rests largely with the order, family, or, in any case, the larger group into which the genus and species fall.

Duplicate entry of this type is often used where this reasoning is inapplicable, and where the very amount and character of the material would justify subdivision by place. In the following examples, which represent current practice, it may be questioned whether the first heading should not be subdivided by place and the second one dispensed with, particularly in view of the fact that the first heading is invariably connected with the second by means of a "see also" reference:

1. Education, Higher.
2. Education—U. S.
   or
2. Universities and colleges—U. S.

1. Education, Secondary.
2. Education—U. S.

Probably the clearest justification for duplicate entry is found in those instances where a subject distinctly represents a dual interest which can be adequately satisfied by duplicate entry, but much less so by any type of subdivision. To this category belong, for example, names of orders, classes, etc., of parasites which infest a particular host. These require entry under both the name of the parasite and the heading *Parasites—[Host]*, *e. g.*, for tapeworms which are parasites of man, 1. *Tapeworms* and 2. *Parasites—Man;* for the nematodes of sheep, 1. *Nematoda* and 2. *Parasites—Sheep*.

IX. Subject Headings vs. Author and Added Entry Headings

Subject or Author? Offhand the difference between author entry and subject entry would appear to be so clear and unequivocal that no discussion of it is necessary. However, a closer examination of rules of author entry and of the relation between author entries and subject entries under the rules reveals that in some respects the line between author and subject entry cannot be clearly drawn. This is due in part to the concept of authorship under the Anglo-American code [1] and in part to the uses to which the two kinds of entry are put.

In effect, the rules for author entry prescribe entry under headings which are not names of persons or of corporate bodies, hence, would not be thought to be authors by the great majority of readers. In this category are the following types of headings:

1) Names of political jurisdictions (countries, provinces, states, counties, cities, and the like) when followed by a form subhead, such as: *Laws, statutes, etc.*; *Treaties, etc.*; *Constitution*; *Charters*; *Ordinances, etc.*

> **U. S.** *Laws, statutes, etc.*
> **Canada.** *Treaties, etc.*
> **Switzerland.** *Constitution.*
> **New Orleans.** *Charters.*
> **Cleveland.** *Ordinances, etc.*

It can be argued that a political jurisdiction is analogous to a corporate body. However, it is unlikely that a reader would discriminate between **U. S.** *Constitution*, in which the United States may be considered the jurisdiction analogous to corporate author, and the phrase "United States Constitution," which could not conceivably be regarded by the reader as an author heading. This is even more obvious in those instances where the name of a people or tribe is used in the manner of the name of a political jurisdiction, *e. g.*, **Hittites.** *Laws, statutes, etc.*

2) Names of denominations and religious orders entered under conventional names as contrasted with official names of religious bodies.

It is not too difficult to conceive of the "Catholic Church" or "Presbyterian Church in the U. S. A." as author, but "Baptists," as contrasted with names of Baptist church bodies, is hardly to be thought of

---

[1] This term is used for the rules compiled originally by committees of the American Library Association and the (British) Library Association and, in the main, represents the common practice of American and British libraries.

as an author, nor, for that matter, are such collective headings as "Congregational churches," especially when followed by a form subhead, *e. g.*, **Congregational churches.** *Liturgy and ritual.*

3) Names of institutions which are used both for the institution and for its physical plant.

"New York Hospital" and "New York. Riverside Church" are not likely to be thought of as authors, yet under the Anglo-American code they would be considered the authors of reports, handbooks, and the like, issued under their authority.

4) Names of ships, used as main entry headings for admiralty proceedings in which the ships are involved, ships' logs, accounts of expeditions named for the ship or known by the ship's name.

Author headings of this type are in the main quite like subject-form headings in that they are used to bring together a particular *kind* of publication. Laws of a country are brought together under the name of the country followed by *Laws, statutes, etc.*, and liturgical works of a denomination under the name of the denomination followed by the subhead *Liturgy and ritual,* in the same manner that encyclopedias are brought together under the subject heading *Encyclopedias and dictionaries* and yearbooks in a particular subject under the name of the subject followed by the subdivision *Yearbooks.* In part, but in a very real sense, the above author headings are used to cover material about the country and the denomination respectively. The main entry heading actually takes the place of a subject-form heading. Such titles must be brought under a subject control in the catalog similar to that provided for entries under personal names and under corporate headings of a more obvious kind, so that all material in the catalog on a given subject could be reached through an appropriate subject heading. However, since it would be a duplication to enter each of the titles bearing a given main entry heading under the same subject heading, economy of space in the catalog suggests the substitution of a reference from the appropriate subject to the author heading. Thus, texts of the Constitution of the United States could be brought out in the catalog under the subject heading *U. S.—Constitutional law*, but, what is better and more economical of space, could be referred to under its main entry heading from that subject, *e. g.*,

> U. S.—Constitutional law
> *see also*
> **U. S.** *Constitution*

Similarly, a code of Hittite law requires subject entry under *Law, Hittite*, or a "see also" reference from *Law, Hittite* to the main entry heading **Hittites.** *Laws, statutes, etc.* A reference from *Admiralty* with the appropriate country subdivision will direct the reader to names of ships used as author headings for admiralty proceedings of the country. A reference from *Ships* to names of ships used as author headings for ships' logs will guide the reader to the material on the ship in those instances where he is unaware that the name of the ship is the author heading.

Author plus Subject. All modern codes of cataloging recognize entry under the name of the author as basic, that is, they consider it the main entry. It is in the scope of the concept of authorship that they differ. In many codes corporate authorship plays a greater or lesser part. It is the Anglo-American code which has extended the concept to include not only administrative publications of societies and institutions, but also works of subject content (as distinguished from works of the imagination) which are not assignable to one or several personal authors, but are sponsored by a corporate body or are issued under its authority. This includes particularly works issued under the authority of government agencies.

One need not go into the justification of this type of main entry beyond its convenience for various purposes and the advantages it has over its alternative, in many codes, of entry under the title of the publication, frequently a trite, not in any sense memorable, title. Certain types of corporate authorship are, however, not clearly intelligible to the reader in that they are either too involved or are not recognized by him as representing authorship at all. To cite an example, the hearings on the irregularities in the primary and general elections in Pennsylvania in 1926 in which William S. Vare was elected Senator would be readily found under the obvious subject heading *Vare, William Scott*, but it is hardly conceivable that the reader would seek them under the actual author headings used: U. S. *Congress. Senate. Special Committee Investigating Expenditures in Senatorial Primary and General Elections* and U. S. *Congress. Senate. Committee on Privileges and Elections.* Similarly, a work about a park, school, or other institution, which is entered under the name of a public body in charge of the institution, will be sought not under the name of the author, but the name of the institution which is the subject of the work. Thus, rules and regulations regarding Yosemite National Park, promulgated by the United States National Park Service, are likely to be sought under the name of the park rather than under U. S. *National Park Service.*[2]

In a number of other types of author entry (more precisely, of main entry) subject approach is needed either in order to provide more ready and direct access to books or to relate the books to material in the subject field into which they fall. This need is recognized to the point that the rules of author and title entry include instructions or recommendations for supplementing the main or added name entries with subject or subject-form headings. The following categories of books require such subject or subject-form entry:

1) Anonymous classics.

   When the titles of anonymous classics involve personal names of real persons, subject entry should be made under the name of the person.

---

[2] *Cf.* rule above (p. 62) for names of institutions used both for the institution and for its physical plant.

Main entry heading: **Richard Cœur de Lion** (*Romance*)
Subject heading: Richard I, King of England, 1157–1199—Poetry.

Main entry heading: **Godly Queene Hester.**
Subject heading: Esther, Queen of Persia—Drama.

This rule may be extended to names of fictitious persons where there is a choice between added entry under the name of a cycle of anonymous classics diversely named and a subject heading, *e. g.*, *Perceval* (*Romances, etc.*) as an assembling subject heading for the anonymous classics **Perceval of Galles** and **Perlesvaus.**

Anonymous classics and sacred books generally do not require subject headings of this sort. However, when they are examples of a particular literary form, or constitute a part of the literature of a certain body of knowledge, a "see also" reference from the appropriate subject or subject-form heading to the uniform heading is necessary.

Buddha and Buddhism—Sacred books
see also
Tripiṭaka
Vinayapiṭaka
Suttapiṭaka

2) Correspondence and letters.

When a collection of letters of a single writer is accompanied by biographical matter, there is a choice of entry between the author of the letters and the author of the biography, the latter being preferred. If the entry is under the biographer, subject entry under the author of the letters is required.

3) Manuscripts and facsimiles of manuscripts.

The author entry of manuscripts and facsimiles of manuscripts conforms to the same rules of entry as books; however, a subject-form heading is required on the following pattern: *Manuscripts,* [*Language*] or *Manuscripts,* [*Language*]—*Facsimiles, e. g., Manuscripts, French* or *Manuscripts, French—Facsimiles.*

4) Atlases.

In view of the fact that, under the rules for author entry, atlases may be entered under a variety of authors (cartographers, publishers, government bureaus, societies, and institutions) and the fact that readers are not always aware of, or interested in, the author of an atlas, general atlases are brought together under the subject-form heading *Atlases.*

5) Liturgical music.

Musical settings for masses, requiems, and other liturgical pieces require a subject-form heading for the medium as well as for the element of the liturgy, since the interest in them rests, with the exception of settings by important composers, primarily on these grounds. Therefore, the full score of Anton Bruckner's *Te Deum* for chorus and orchestra would require the following headings:

  1. Te Deum laudamus (Music)
  2. Choruses, Sacred.
     or, more precisely,
  2. Choruses, Sacred (Mixed voices, 4 pts.) with orchestra—Scores.

To lead the reader to musical settings to the liturgy of a particular church, a reference should be made to the music heading for the element of the liturgy as follows:

Catholic Church. *Liturgy and ritual. Missal.*

For musical settings of the Mass *see* the subject heading *Masses.*

6) Thematic catalogs.

A thematic catalog of the works of an individual composer is obviously identified with the composer, rather than the compiler, hence should be assigned a subject heading under the name of the composer.

7) Heraldic visitations.

Heraldic visitations, which, by rule, are entered under the name of the herald or king-of-arms, require entry under the heading *Visitations, Heraldic* subdivided by place.

  Visitations, Heraldic—Nottingham, Eng.
  Visitations, Heraldic—London.

8) Collections of examples or reproductions of the graphic arts.

When drawings, engravings, etc., represent the major part of a work, but the accompanying text constitutes a substantial part of it, entry under the author of the text is preferred to entry under the artist, in which case subject entry is made under the artist. This represents, in effect, a choice between entry under artist as author and artist as subject. If main entry is under the author of the text, therefore, the artist constitutes the subject of the text, notwithstanding the presence of the reproductions. Thus, "Augustus Saint-Gaudens" by C. Lewis Hind is entered under **Hind, Charles Lewis**, 1862–1927, and subject entry is made under *Saint-Gaudens, Augustus, 1848–1907*, although the work contains but 47 pages of text and 52 plates.

Illustrations by a single artist of an author's work which are assembled in a separate volume require subject entry under the author's name followed by subdivision *Illustrations*, whether the volume of illustrations is entered under the artist or the writer of the accompanying text. Thus, a volume of Sir J. Noel Paton's illustrations for Shakespeare's "Tempest" would require the subject heading *Shakespeare, William—Illustrations*.

9) Parodies.

Because, under the rules of author entry, parodies are entered under the author of the parody, subject entry under the author and title of the work parodied is clearly indicated. Readers are as likely to seek parodies of a particular work as to seek the work of a particular parodist.

10) Concordances, commentaries, scholia.

Since concordances are entered under the name of the compiler, subject entry should be made under the name of the work concordanced (author and title, or the uniform heading of an anonymous classic or sacred work, or any other heading prescribed by the rules), on the grounds that the reader does not know, or is not concerned with, the name of the compiler of the concordance, his primary interest being in the work concordanced. Commentaries and scholia accompanied by partial or fragmentary text, or text subordinated to the commentary, are clearly entered under the commentator and scholiast, hence, for the same reason as concordances, require subject entry under author and title of the work commentated. In the case of sacred works, as in the case of voluminous personal authors, commentaries require a subject entry under the uniform heading followed by the subdivision *Commentaries*. This applies to commentaries which themselves are entered under uniform headings.

Main entry: **Midrash.**   *Tanḥuma.*
Subject heading: Bible.   O. T.   Pentateuch—Commentaries.

When scholia are entered under the name of an editor, as when the name of the scholiast is unknown, the subject heading consists of the name of the author of the work upon which the scholia are based, followed by the subdivision *Scholia*.

Main entry: **Botschuyver, Hendrik Johan.**
                          Scholia in Horatium . . . edidit . . .
                          dr. H. J. Botschuyver.
Subject heading: Horatius Flaccus, Quintus—Scholia.

11) Festschriften.

Collections of brief scholarly contributions issued in honor of a person, society, or institution on the occasion of an anniversary celebration are entered under the name of the editor, corporate author, or title, under the same rules of entry as other types of collections by various authors. Precisely because they are variously entered, the most accurate way of identifying them is by the name of the person, society, or institution honored. By rule and by almost invariable custom,[3] subject entry is made under that name. Festschriften usually, though not always, contain biographical, critical, and bibliographical contributions relating to the honoree, which is the justification for the use of subject entry. Added entry other than subject entry would not, of course, be justified except where contributions by the honoree are included. Subject entry is invariably made also under the heading, or headings, which cover the subject matter of the festschrift as a whole.

In general, subject entry is indicated, whenever the author entry is based on a concept of authorship with which the average reader is unfamiliar, or when the primary approach on the part of the reader is not through the author entry, an added entry under any other name, or under title, but through the subject of the work.

[3] *A. L. A. Cataloging Rules for Author and Title Entries* (2d ed.; 1949), p. 9, rule 5A (1c).

X. Subject Catalog vs. Shelflist

Besides serving as an inventory record of the library's classified collections, the shelflist can be used, within limits, as a classified, or systematic, catalog. However, as in the case of any classed catalog, it can be approached only through an index of some sort, since it is arranged according to the symbols of the classification system which the library employs. The relative index of the classification and the indexes to its individual parts may be used as an index to the shelflist. To a certain extent the subject headings for the books in the classified collections may also be used for this purpose. The limitations on this use of subject headings point, on the one hand, to the fact that the shelflist as such cannot take the place of the alphabetical subject catalog and, on the other hand, to the possibility of using the shelflist as a complement to the catalog in such a way as to reduce the growth of the catalog without impairing the subject approach to the classified collections.

Since, for the purpose of shelving, only one class number can be assigned to the physical book, the number must obviously represent the subject matter of the book comprehensively, if possible, or the first or major part of the book, if it deals with diverse subjects. In the case of a set of books, that is, a collection of monographs, it may be desirable to keep the set intact, rather than scatter individual monographs throughout the collection by classifying each monograph separately. Classifying it as a collection of monographs is, in fact, inevitable when the complete monograph occupies parts of more than one volume. This limitation does not, however, apply to subject headings. If the subject matter of a book represents a systematic treatment of it and can be expressed by a single term, then one subject heading will cover it adequately. When this is not the case, as many subject headings may be used for the book as the distinct topics treated in it require. A single subject heading may be applied to the collection of monographs, if the collection as a whole represents a comprehensive treatment of a single subject. On the other hand, regardless of the fact that the collection is kept intact on the shelves, as many subject headings may be assigned to it as the individual monographs require.

In view of these facts, it is obvious that the shelflist ordinarily presents under any class number not all the works in the library which deal with the subject to which the number applies, but only those which deal primarily with it and those not included in a collection under a broader number. A full-fledged classed catalog includes entries under as many class numbers as are needed to represent the subjects treated in the physical volume or in the individual monographs in a series kept as a unit on the shelves. A shelflist serves the purpose of a classed catalog only within the limits indicated.

Nevertheless, for a considerable number of books on the library's shelves on any subject there is a direct correspondence between subject heading and class number. Under most broad subject headings many of the books will bear the same class number, for the reason that classification systems provide class numbers for broad treatments of a subject.

If the shelflist is available to the public and is not too far removed from the catalog, a reference from the subject heading to the corresponding class number in the shelflist will take the place of many entries, yet guide the reader to most of the material on the subject. It will, furthermore, give the reader an insight into the significance of the number. The reference must, however, be worded to show clearly that only part of the material is to be found in the shelflist and that the rest is entered under the same heading immediately following the reference.

There are areas of subject matter, such as sports, in which specific topics are most frequently treated in detached monographs rather than in encyclopedic works or series. The correspondence between subject heading and class number is very nearly complete. The use of a reference to the shelflist in such instances is, however, to be limited to topics on which the number of books is large, since the only justification for directing the reader to the shelflist is economy in the preparation of entries and of space in the catalog.

The following examples will illustrate the use of a reference from the subject heading to a class number in the shelflist both for broad subjects and specific topics.

Geology—Uruguay.

For works devoted exclusively to this subject as a whole, *see*, in addition to those cited under this heading, the following number in the shelflist:

QE249

Skating.

For works on this subject, *see*, in addition to those cited under this heading, the following number in the shelflist:

GV849

An examination of the entries under the headings *Geology—Uruguay* and *Skating* will show that few of the entries bear class numbers other than QE249 and GV849 respectively. Those that do bear other class numbers are either analytical, that is, they cover parts of books, or articles in periodicals, or are used for works in which the given subject heading is a secondary one, the classification being based on another, more important aspect of the work.

At the Library of Congress the device of referring from subject heading to class number was used to a limited extent before the shelflist and the public catalog were placed so far apart that access to the shelflist on the part of the public became difficult. The device of referring to the shelflist does emphasize the relationship between subject heading and class number and represents one way of reducing the large number of entries under some headings without eliminating the reader's approach to them altogether.

XI. Subject Headings in Special Library Catalogs

The basic principles underlying the choice of terms and the form of subject headings in the catalog of a general library are, broadly speaking, equally applicable to the special library, whether the special library serves a particular subject interest or a particular clientele. Since, however, the collections of special libraries are usually limited to a single subject, however broad, and since the clientele they serve is frequently, or in considerable part, made up of specialists, that is, persons of special interest and competence, the approach of the reader to the subject catalog differs in some respects from that of the general public, hence, makes deviation from these principles desirable in certain respects. Some of these deviations are applicable to catalogs of special libraries as a whole, while others vary with the subject field and the level of specialization of the clientele of the library.

A considerable number of the headings in any subject field consist of the name of the subject or begin with its adjectival form, *e. g.*, *Chemistry, Inorganic; Chemistry—Laboratory manuals; Chemical apparatus; Chemical elements*. In a chemical library, the term "laboratory manuals" obviously refers to laboratory manuals in chemistry, the term "apparatus" to chemical apparatus, and "elements" to the chemical elements. Hence, it is unnecessary in many instances to begin headings with the noun designating the subject or the adjective derived from it. Unless the noun, or adjective, is so intimately a part of the heading that the heading would have little or no meaning without it, it may well be omitted in the special library catalog. *Laboratory manuals* would suffice in place of *Chemistry—Laboratory manuals*, and *Elements* in place of *Chemical elements*. On the other hand, *Chemical engineering* cannot be reduced, since *Engineering* would convey, even in a chemical library, the notion of engineering as a whole, rather than chemical engineering specifically. Similarly, in a music library catalog, *Manuals, text-books, etc.*, could take the place of *Music—Manuals, text-books, etc.*, and *Instruments* the place of *Musical instruments*, while *Musical glasses* would lose its meaning if reduced to *Glasses*.

Following the same reasoning, the name of a place used as subdivision under the major subject may be used as the main heading, qualified or subdivided, if necessary, by the name of the subject. Thus, in an agricultural library, *United States* will bring together works dealing with agriculture as a whole in the United States; in a music library, the name of the place, by itself or with *Music* as a subdivision, will serve a similar purpose. General references will guide the reader, in such instances, to lesser topics in the field with the same place connotation.

73

U. S.—Agriculture.

See also other subjects in the field of agriculture with the subdivision U. S., *e. g.*, Fruit-culture—U. S., Vegetable gardening—U. S.

France—Music.

See also Music, French *and other subjects in the field of music with the subdivision* France, *e. g.*, Church music—France, Symphony orchestras—France.

In a geographic library, or, in general, where the demand for material in a special library is primarily on a geographic basis, place can, of course, be used as the primary heading with subdivision by the broad headings in the major subject field. This would apply only to headings which have a definite place connotation, so that, in a general library catalog, place is used as subdivision under subject.

Where the name of the subject is used solely as a qualifying term to distinguish between different meanings of the term, it can be omitted in a special library catalog. By way of example, *Composition (Music)* can be reduced to simply *Composition* in a music library catalog, since the latter would be used in the sense of musical composition and the qualification can be reserved, if necessary, for *Composition (Art)*, and *Composition (Law)*, the latter having a totally different sense.

Where the name of the subject is used in a compound heading in juxtaposition to the name of another subject, the order of the two should be reversed, if possible, in order to give prominence to the less obvious subject. In a medical library, the heading *Medicine and art* would read *Art and medicine*, and, in a music library, *Architecture and music* would take the place of the usual form of the heading *Music and architecture*.

In the case of inverted headings where the qualifying term is a geographic or ethnic adjective, inversion accomplishes a grouping of those phases of the subject which have a geographic and ethnic significance and also their separation from other aspects of the subject. Inversion can be retained for this purpose even in a special library catalog. However, access to the subject with reference to a particular place or ethnic group is made simple and direct, if the direct order is used. *Music, Jewish* and *Music, African* thus become *Jewish music* and *African music* in a music library catalog. Similarly, *Primitive music* takes the place of *Music, Primitive* and *Popular music* the place of *Music, Popular*.

Biological Headings. In certain subject fields, the language of the heading in the special library catalog plays a distinctly different role from that in a general library catalog. Names of genera and species in biological science, for example, are preferably given in Latin or Romanized Greek, making them more precisely identifiable, *e. g.*, *Lycopodium* in place of *Club-mosses*, *Strigiformes* in place of *Owls*. For that reason, if the scientific terminology of a subject is officially, or by universal acceptance, in a foreign language, the special library is justified in using it in preference to popular terms in English. References from the English synonyms should be in the usual form of a "see" reference for terms which are completely synonymous; otherwise, the English term from which the reference is made should be properly qualified. A general library would use *Redwood* for the *Sequoia sempervirens* and *Sequoia* for the *Sequoia gigantea*. In a botanical library, entry under the Latin name would conform to usage in the professional literature of the botanist and would bring the two species of the genus *Sequoia* together. The following references would be necessary:

> Redwood
> > *see*
> Sequoia sempervirens
>
> Big tree (Sequoia gigantea)
> > *see*
> Sequoia gigantea
>
> Giant sequoia
> > *see*
> Sequoia gigantea

While in the catalog of a general library "see also" references are required from *Redwood* to *Sequoia* (the name for the big tree used in the catalog) and from *Sequoia* to *Redwood*, there is no need for references from one species to the other in a botanical library, since both headings begin with the name of the genus.

In a scientific library, it is of considerable importance to bring together in the catalog, and give prominence to, the more recent literature of the subject. To use period subdivisions, such as, say, *20th century* or *1920–*, would achieve the purpose of bringing together the newer material. Under the commonly accepted principles of filing, the headings with these subdivisions would follow those without subdivision, hence the use of period subdivisions like the above would relegate the newer works to a position following the older works. This can be obviated either by revising the headings already in the catalog and assigning to the older work a subdivision *To 1900* or *To 1920*, or, the more common method, by adding the date of publication in the upper right hand corner of the entry, following the heading, and filing the entries in reverse chronological order. While these methods are feasible, the second, which is in actual use in library catalogs, presents a problem in filing and in the fullest use of the catalog. The filing problem arises out of the fact that arrangement is in reverse numerical order of years of publication, requiring special instructions to the reader as well as the filer. The fullest use of the catalog is interfered with, since this arrangement makes it impossible to use the subject approach as a means of finding a particular entry when the name of the author is a common one or there is doubt in regard to its form and spelling, as in the case of a text on photomicrography by "someone named Johnson," which is easier to find under the heading *Photomicrography* than by looking under the hundreds of entries under "Johnson." Furthermore, this device separates various editions of the same work, even where two or three successive editions might serve the reader's purpose equally well.

Chemical Headings. Whereas, in a general library catalog, chemical compounds are entered under their commonly accepted names, which are, in many instances, the trade names used in commerce and industry, the needs of a chemical library are such that it is best to enter them in accord with an accepted system of nomenclature, such as that developed by the Nomenclature Committee of the Chemical Society of London and the American Chemical Society; the Nomenclature, Spelling and Pronunciation Committee of the American Chemical Society; and the Committee on the Reform of the Nomenclature of Organic Chemistry of the International Union of Chemistry. As an example of the difference in choice of heading between a general and a chemical library, "salt" as the synonym of "sodium chloride" would be entered under the heading *Salt* in a general library, but under *Sodium chloride* in a chemical library, where it will stand with the names of other sodium compounds; similarly, a chemical library would use *Carbonyl chloride* in place of *Phosgene,* and *Methyl alcohol* or *Methanol* in place of *Wood alcohol.*

Names of compounds which indicate the oxidation state of the compound, *e. g.*, nitrous oxide, ferric sulphate, are so entered in a general catalog. A chemical library may choose to enter them, in the manner of "Chemical Abstracts," under the name based on the constituents, without reference to the oxidation state, *e. g.*, *Iron sulphates* in place of *Ferric sulphate* and *Ferrous sulphate; Nitrogen oxides* in place of *Nitrous oxide, Nitric oxide, Nitrogen dioxide, Nitrogen trioxide, Nitrogen tetroxide,* and *Nitrogen pentoxide.*

Double salts are entered in a general catalog under the form most often encountered in chemical literature, a "see" reference guiding the reader to the form chosen from the name with the anions, or cations, reversed, *e. g.*,

Magnesium ammonium phosphate.

Ammonium magnesium phosphate
see
Magnesium ammonium phosphate

In a chemical library, it may be desirable to make entry under both forms. Duplicate entry would be justified in that it would bring together the salts of each metal.

It is inevitable that there should be little consistency in the treatment of names of alloys in either general or chemical library catalogs, since the literature reveals a lack of consistency in the order of the names of the constituents. Chromium-iron-nickel alloys, for example, are referred to in the literature indiscriminately as chromium-iron-nickel alloys, iron-nickel-chromium alloys, and nickel-chromium-iron alloys. Obviously, a single form is to be chosen, whether based on the form first encountered in cataloging or the alphabetic order of the English names of the metals. The latter has been the preferred usage in general library catalogs, "see also" references being provided from the headings for the alloys of each metal involved, *e. g.*,

> Iron alloys
> *see also*
> Chromium-iron-nickel alloys

> Chromium alloys
> *see also*
> Chromium-iron-nickel alloys

> Nickel alloys
> *see also*
> Chromium-iron-nickel alloys

Special libraries may prefer to omit entry under the name of the specific alloy, using instead the headings for the alloys of each metal, these being in the example used above, *Iron alloys, Chromium alloys*, and *Nickel alloys*. These broader headings may each be subdivided by each of the other metals in the alloy, *e. g., Iron alloys—Chromium, Iron alloys—Nickel, Chromium alloys—Iron*, etc.

In a general catalog the name of an individual compound beginning with the prefix "meta-," "ortho-," or "para-" is entered under the part of the name following the prefix, unless the name is applied to an industrial product or is popularly applied to the compound in its prefix form. In a special library catalog, the heading may be used in inverted form with the prefix following the heading. For the special library catalog a general "see" reference should be made from the prefix as follows:

> Ortho—
> *See the compound to the name of which* Ortho- *is prefixed, e. g.,*
> Tolidine *for Orthotolidine,* Cymene *for Orthocymene.*

Music Headings. Subject headings in a music catalog conform, with reference to inversion, metathesis, and the omission of the initial noun or adjective, or of the qualifying word, to the rules which apply to special library catalogs. *Inventions and patents, Musical* in lieu of the *Musical inventions and patents* of the general catalog; *Literature and music* in lieu of *Music and literature; Intervals and scales* in lieu of *Musical intervals and scales; Composition* in lieu of *Composition (Music)*. Because of the special character of the collections of a music library, which include not only books about music but music scores as well, music subject headings present characteristics which are found in other fields in a much smaller degree, if at all.

Music subject headings must distinguish between works describing a particular musical form and examples of that musical form. This is accomplished by the use of the singular for works dealing with the musical form and the plural for compositions in that form.

> Sonata *and* Sonatas
> Chorale *and* Chorales
> Tarantella *and* Tarantellas

The less frequent use of this device in other fields is illustrated by *Short story*, which is used for works on the short story as a literary form and *Short stories* used for collections of short stories. The plural, when used for examples of particular literary or musical form, represents not a subject heading in the narrow sense of the word, but a form subject, or form heading, essentially like the heading *Encyclopedias and dictionaries* or *Almanacs*, under which are entered entries for individual examples of a kind of publication, rather than books about the subject named in the heading.

Music headings must take account of the characteristics of compositions upon which their performance depends. Thus, in the case of instrumental ensembles, the kind and number of instruments must be indicated and whether the music was originally written for the particular ensemble or an arrangement, whether the work consists of the full score, the parts only, or the score and the parts. In the case of choral compositions, sacred and secular choruses must be distinguished and indication given of the kind of accompaniment (or whether unaccompanied), and whether for men's or women's or mixed voices.

In general, music presents a dualism which determines the character of the form headings. Musical compositions may be regarded from the point of view of the musical form which they represent or the medium to be used in performing them. For example, piano concertos may be entered either as concertos or piano music. A library must decide which approach its clientele usually, or most frequently, employs. If the choice falls, as in the headings developed in the Library of Congress, on the musical form, then the heading must indicate the medium as a specification following the form and a "see also" reference must be made from the heading used for the medium; if, however, all the compositions for a given medium were brought together under a heading representing the medium, some device, such as subdivision by musical form with references from the heading for the musical form to the heading adopted, or duplicate entry under both medium and form, must be employed. Library of Congress practice may be illustrated as follows:

> Concertos (Piano)
>
> (with "see also" references from *Piano music* and *Piano with orchestra*)
>
> Sonatas (2 flutes)
>
> (with a "see also" reference from *Flute music (2 flutes)*)

Sonatas (Viola and harpsichord)

(with a "see" reference from *Sonatas (Harpsichord and viola)* and a "see also" reference from *Viola and harpsichord music*)

In those instances where the compositions are named for the size of the ensemble and the kinds of instruments, the heading will obviously express the medium, making references necessary solely from the headings for the individual instruments involved, *e. g., String quartets*, with "see also" references from *Viola music, Violin music,* and *Violoncello music.*

Finally, it must be borne in mind that, except for the variations of the type mentioned, subject headings in a special library catalog are fundamentally like headings in a general library catalog, in that they must be as specific as the subject matter of the books requires and language makes possible and that the terms chosen should by all means be those which represent current usage among those who write and those who seek information on the subject.

XII. Filing Problems

The filing of subject entries, whether in an alphabetical subject catalog or a dictionary catalog, presents a variety of problems due, in the first instance, to necessary disregard of, or deviation from, the alphabetic order, and, in the second instance, to the necessity for determining the best or most useful order of entries where alphabetic order is not involved at all, as, for instance, in the case of entries of several kinds having the same or closely similar headings.

Alphabetical Filing. Alphabetical filing has reached a high degree of uniformity in American library catalogs, which makes it possible to speak of certain filing practices as universal insofar as they affect the filing of subject entries in a card catalog. These rules can be stated in the following terms:

1. Entries are arranged word by word, the alphabeting proceeding letter by letter to the end of each word. Some catalogs and works of reference which are alphabetically arranged follow the practice of alphabeting letter by letter without regard to the end of the word, a practice which results in a different arrangement of entries from that found in most library catalogs.

Word by word	*Letter by letter*
New Amsterdam	New Amsterdam
New York	Newark
Newark	New York

   As a corollary to this rule, the shorter of two words is filed ahead of the longer one which includes all of the first, *e. g.*,

America	Cortin. [subject]
American	Cortina, Alfonso.
Americana	Cortinarius. [subject]

   and, by the same token, a simple heading is filed preceding its subdivisions or the same heading followed by qualification or extensions of any kind.

   Art.
   Art—Dictionaries.
   Art, Abstract.
   Art industries and trade.

2. When the same word or phrase is used as main or added entry and as subject, the order is: 1) main entry, 2) added entry, 3) subject.

> Orange, Conn.   [as author]
> Orange, Conn.   [as added entry]
> Orange, Conn.   [as subject]

3. When the same word or phrase is used as a personal name (*i. e.*, a surname), the name of a place, a subject, or the title of a book, the relative order of entries is as given.

> Reading, Geoffrey.
> Reading, Eng.
> Reading.   [subject]
> Reading: a vice or a virtue?   [title]

4. Entries are arranged alphabetically in the order of the letters of the English alphabet regardless of the language of the entry. Thus, *ch*, even in Spanish words, follows *cg* and precedes *ci*, whereas in the Spanish alphabet it follows *cz*. Similarly, those consonants in foreign languages using roman characters which bear diacritical marks, or are otherwise modified, are filed in the order of the corresponding English letters without regard for the diacritical marks, *e. g.*, Polish *l* is filed as *l*, Spanish *ñ* as *n*, and *ç* as *c*.

> *Note:* Modified vowels, however, are filed variously by American libraries. In Library of Congress practice modified vowels in all languages are filed as though they were umlauted and the umlaut expressed by letters rather than diacritical signs; thus, *ä, ö, ü*, are filed as *ae, oe, ue*, respectively, *ø* as *oe, å* as *aa*.

Nonalphabetic Filing. Whereas filing under these rules is primarily alphabetic, in some respects it deviates from the alphabetic order either in the interest of a more effective use of the catalog or to meet the requirements of logic. The very arrangement of entries letter by letter within each word in a sense violates alphabetic order, but it helps to keep related headings together. Thus, by virtue of this rule, the headings relating to color which begin with the word "color" stand together in the catalog, whereas, if arranged strictly alphabetically, that is, in the order of the letters of the heading and without regard to word length, the order in the catalog would be as in the following example:

Strictly alphabetically	*Word by word*
Color.	Color.
Colorado River.	Color photography.
Color photography.	Colorado River.

The effect of mixing unrelated words in strictly alphabetical filing is increased, if the subdivisions of a subject are not filed immediately following the subject.

Strictly alphabetically	*Word by word*
Color.	Color.
Colorado River.	Color—Analysis.
Color—Analysis.	Color—Physiological effect.
Color-blindness.	Color—Study and teaching.
Colored Methodist Episcopal Church.	Color-blindness.
Coloring matter.	Color of plants.
Color of plants.	Color-sense.
Color—Physiological effect.	Colorado River.
Color-sense.	Colored Methodist Episcopal Church.
Colors, Liturgical.	Coloring matter.
Color—Study and teaching.	Colors, Liturgical.

As seen from the above example, filing word by word and filing the subject subdivisions immediately following the subject brings everything dealing with the subject *Color* as such together, while other headings beginning with the word "color" and bearing a direct relationship to the subject immediately follow the subdivisions. On the other hand, filing strictly in the order of the letters of the headings scatters *Colorado River, Colored Methodist Episcopal Church*, and *Colors, Liturgical*, totally unrelated headings, among the subdivisions of *Color*.

Chronological Order. In any subject catalog there are several types of headings which involve filing by period or date. The most obvious use of chronological filing is in period subdivisions under the headings for the history of a country. This applies equally where the period is named and where actual dates are given. The chronological arrangement follows the *opening* date of the periods. Where several periods beginning with the same date are used, the most inclusive period would come first and be followed by the others in the order of inclusiveness.

> U. S.—History—Colonial period.
> U. S.—History—King William's War, 1689–1697.
> U. S.—History—Queen Anne's War, 1702–1713.
> U. S.—History—King George's War, 1744–1748.
> U. S.—History—French and Indian War, 1755–1763.
> U. S.—History—Revolution.
> U. S.—History—1783–1865.
> U. S.—History—Confederation, 1783–1789.
> U. S.—History—Constitutional period, 1789–1809.
> U. S.—History—Whisky Insurrection, 1794. *See*
>   Whisky Insurrection, 1794.
> U. S.—History—War with France, 1798–1800.
> U. S.—History—Tripolitan War, 1801–1805.
> U. S.—History—1809–1817.
> U. S.—History—War of 1812.
> U. S.—History—1815–1861.

U. S.—History—War with Algeria, 1815.
U. S.—History—War with Mexico, 1845–1848.
U. S.—History—1849–1877.
U. S.—History—Civil War.
U. S.—History—1865–
U. S.—History—1898–
U. S.—History—War of 1898.
U. S.—History—20th century.
U. S.—History—1933–1945.

Order of Subdivisions. The clearest departure from alphabetical filing is found in the grouping of different types of subdivisions under a given heading and in the arrangement of headings with different categories of qualifying terms. Many libraries attempt to file alphabetically word by word disregarding semantic or structural relationships between subdivisions and qualifying terms of different kinds. In Library of Congress practice, however, structure, semantics, and logic enter in to a considerable extent. The order of subdivisions in the Library of Congress catalogs is as follows: 1) form subdivisions, that is, those which relate to the bibliographic form or, in general, the kind or form of the subject matter; 2) time subdivisions, where they occur as direct subdivisions of the subject, rather than as divisions under *History;* 3) geographic subdivisions; and 4) inverted headings (so-called "comma" inversions), in which the inversion serves as a kind of subdivision.

Art.
Art—Addresses, essays, lectures.
Art—History.
Art—History—20th century.
Art—Yearbooks.
Art—20th century.   *See* Art—History—20th century.
Art—Belgium.
Art—Leipzig.
Art—Pennsylvania.
Art—Yugoslavia.
Art, American.
Art, Ancient.
Art, Baroque.
Art, Belgian.
Art, Decorative.
Art, Mohammedan.
Art, Pennsylvania German.
Art, Yugoslav.

The headings *Art—Addresses, essays, lectures* through *Art—Yearbooks* belong to the group of form subdivisions; the reference from *Art—20th century* finds its place, as a time subdivision, between the form and the place subdivisions; the headings *Art—Belgium* through *Art—Yugoslavia* form the group of place subdivisions (*Art—Leipzig* being evidence that place subdivision under the heading *Art* is direct); and the miscellany of inverted headings beginning with *Art, American* fall with the last group.   If these headings were filed alphabetically, they would arrange themselves as follows:

> Art.
> Art—Addresses, essays, lectures.
> Art, American.
> Art, Ancient.
> Art, Baroque.
> Art, Belgian.
> Art—Belgium.
> Art, Decorative.
> Art—History.
> Art—History—20th century.
> Art—Leipzig.
> Art, Mohammedan.
> Art—Pennsylvania.
> Art, Pennsylvania German.
> Art—20th century.   *See* Art—History—20th century.
> Art—Yearbooks.
> Art, Yugoslav.
> Art—Yugoslavia.

Whereas the grouping of the headings in Library of Congress practice can be justified, the order of the groups is inevitably arbitrary.   It is doubtful whether most readers are aware of the order of groups, even when they find the headings they seek or can discriminate between subdivision (in the so-called "dash" headings) and inversion (in the so-called "comma" headings).

Position of References.   The relative position of "see also" references in relation to the heading from which the references are made presents an almost insoluble problem, hence, one to which a variety of solutions have been adopted by different libraries.   "See also" references from a given heading to related headings of the same order and to subordinate headings can be filed rationally only on the basis of the heading from which the reference is made.   It would not make sense to file it secondarily by the words "*see also*," since it would then interfile with the author or title main entry heading.   Should, then, the references precede all the entries under the given subject heading, a practice followed by some libraries?   Should they follow the simple subject heading but precede the subdivision of the heading, as is done in the Library of Congress?   Should the references follow the heading and all its form and place subdivisions—its "dash" subdivisions—as is done in a number of libraries?   There is a fourth possibility, that of placing the references following even the inverted (or "comma") headings, although there is no evidence that this is followed, the possibility being limited to libraries which file the four types of heading illustrated above in a single alphabet. The following examples illustrate the four possible positions of the references with respect to the headings.

1.   Glassware, *see also* Cut glass; Lamp-chimneys, globes, etc.
      Glassware.
      Glassware—Catalogs.
      Glassware—Spain.
      Glassware, Oriental.

2.   Glassware.
      Glassware, *see also* Cut glass; Lamp-chimneys, globes, etc.
      Glassware—Catalogs.
      Glassware—Spain.
      Glassware, Oriental.
      > This group of examples represents the order of the references and entries in the Library of Congress catalogs.

3.   Glassware.
      Glassware—Catalogs.
      Glassware—Spain.
      Glassware, *see also* Cut glass; Lamp-chimneys, globes, etc.
      Glassware, Oriental.
      > The order represented by this group is used in many libraries.

4.   Glassware.
      Glassware—Catalogs.
      Glassware—Spain.
      Glassware, Oriental.
      Glassware, *see also* Cut glass; Lamp-chimneys, globes, etc.

The purpose of the "see also" references being to guide the reader to related material in the library and to indicate to him that subjects of more limited scope are to be found under specific headings, it is obvious that the references must somehow be so placed in the catalog that the reader who finds the heading will also find the references. It is inconceivable that the reader would, without being aware of the several types of headings and their order in the catalog, find the references except possibly where the references come first. However, even that possibility is based on an assumption, not warranted in fact, that the reader always begins his search with the first entries under a given heading.

A solution which presents itself as being most likely to attract the attention of the reader to the references is one which does not depend on the relative order of references and the several types of entries, but which gives the references physical prominence in the catalog. It would achieve its ends by exalting the tabbed guide-card to the level of a vehicle of information on the use of the card catalog. The tab would bear the heading, the body of the tabbed card providing, first, a statement giving the order of the groups of subdivisions and of the headings followed by qualifying terms, and, second, the references to related headings.

ART

The entries on this subject are arranged alphabetically in groups as follows:

1) *Art* (Works on the subject as a whole);

2) *Art* followed by a subdivision indicating the kind of publication or a phase of the subject, *e. g., Art—History; Art—Periodicals;*

3) *Art* followed by the name of a country, city, and the like;

4) *Art* followed by an adjective indicating a school or kind of art, a period, etc., *e. g., Art, Ancient; Art, Baroque; Art, British;*

5) *Art* as part of a phrase, *e. g., Art and war; Art centers; Art patronage.*

 Continued on next card

ART

(Card 2)

See also

Anatomy, Artistic
Animals in art
Architecture
Arts and crafts movement
Bronzes
Christian art and symbolism
Cubism
Decoration and ornament
Drawing
Engraving
Etching

Folk art
Human figure in art
Illumination of books
    and manuscripts
Impressionism (Art)
Miniature painting
Mosaics
Mural painting and decoration
Post-impressionism (Art)
Posters
Sculpture

If necessary, the tabbed guide-cards could be made to draw the attention of the reader by the use of a distinctive, bright color, or by adding, following the heading, some such phrase as "Instructions to user" or "Arrangement of entries."

Interfiling in a Dictionary Catalog. The basic rules of filing common to American libraries take cognizance of the problem of interfiling subject entries with other kinds of entries in the dictionary catalog. Where different types of entry have the same heading, their order must be determined arbitrarily. Two of the areas of arbitrary arrangement are covered by the sequences: author (name entry)-added entry-subject and person-place-subject-title. In general, author entry traditionally occupies first place in catalogs, since authorship is the primary element in the identification of a work. Added entry frequently represents a kind of alternate authorship, hence precedes all entries except author entries. A subject heading being constant in its phrasing takes precedence of the fortuitous and variable wording of titles. Libraries avoid the use of titles which have the same wording as subject headings or subject references, except in the case of titles of works of the imagination since the latter have little or no subject value.

The problem of interfiling of subject entries with other types of entry is illustrated by the following examples of actual headings:

> **Fife, Clyde Lee.**
> Fife, John Priestley, joint author. [added entry for work entered under Moxley, D   J.]
> **Fife, Scotland.** *Sheriff court.* [author entry]
> Fife, Scotland—Antiquities.
> Fife. [subject]
> Fife—Instruction and study.
> Fife and drum. [title added entry for work by Lascelles Wraxall]
> **Fife Mounted Volunteer Rifle Corps.** *See* **Gt. Brit.** *Army. 1st Fife-shire Light Horse Volunteer Corps.*
> Fife music. [subject]

XIII. Procedures and Personnel

Lists of Headings—How Complete? The source of subject headings to which catalogers usually turn is some recognized general list or one limited to the field of knowledge in which the subject matter of the book in hand falls. Other things being equal, this is properly the first step to take. If the heading sought is found in a general, widely-accepted list, the cataloger has some assurance that the term chosen has been carefully considered, fitted into the system of headings represented by the list, and provided with appropriate references.

It should be borne in mind, however, that, unlike classification systems, lists of subject headings do not necessarily provide equally for all fields of knowledge, since they include as a rule only such headings as the library which has issued the list has had occasion to apply to books it has added to its collections. A system of classification must fit all fields of knowledge into a pattern and must develop them to the same degree of specificity. Hence, it provides for all contributions to knowledge, if not on the basis of their specific content, then at least broadly on the basis of the body of subject matter of which they form a part. To try to accomplish the same thing for subject headings would be both impractical and unwise.

Since one of the values of an alphabetical subject catalog lies in the specificity of its headings, a complete list of subject headings even in a single subject field is next to impossible to prepare, since it would involve recording all known ideas, objects, processes, and relationships of the subject area. It would be a stupendous undertaking, and a futile one, to name all branches of chemistry, all chemical elements and their isotopes, all compounds and their isomers, all alloys, all types of reactions, all laboratory and industrial procedures and processes, all apparatus, appliances, and machinery in the field, all relationships of chemistry as a whole and of its branches, including applications to other fields! Only a minute part of the product would be required by any library no matter how large or how specialized. Furthermore, in any growing field of knowledge new concepts and objects and changes in terminology would make a list of this sort obsolete in a relatively short time. It is true that in some fields an approach to completeness and definitiveness would be easier to achieve, and the task would not be so great. Yet even there—as, for example, in mathematics, history, or literature—the need for change would in time render a large share of the effort useless.

Sources of New Headings. Since all existing lists are limited to such headings as have been devised to cover actual books, pamphlets, and articles in periodicals found in a particular library (or in a group of libraries), even relatively small

89

libraries and, particularly, special libraries find it necessary to establish new headings for their own catalogs. This need arises from two circumstances: no list is complete enough and sufficiently up-to-the-minute to keep up with the increase of knowledge, and no list is adequate to the needs of a library when the library undertakes to catalog parts of collected works or articles in periodicals not previously cataloged by the library issuing the list or by cooperative cataloging enterprises.

Choosing the proper heading and determining which references should be made from and to the chosen heading require, in many instances, special competence in the field in which the subject matter lies. Admittedly, any well-educated cataloger can frequently, with a small amount of effort, determine through works of reference and the current literature of the field what is the best term for the topic to be covered and, with a lesser degree of competence, can make the necessary connections, by means of references, with related topics in the catalog.

This is not always possible, however, in the sciences, in philosophy, theology, law, music, and probably also in economics and the other social sciences. There a familiarity with the subject and its terminology is necessary, the kind and degree of familiarity acquired through constant study and reading of current literature on the subject. Even if the level of education of the cataloger is such as to make the literature of the subject intelligible to him, establishing the necessary subject heading calls for far more time-consuming searching through works of reference and current periodicals than would be required of the subject specialist. Furthermore, the results achieved by the layman are frequently subject to question on the score of his lack of competence in the field, whereas the specialist is expected to have the necessary knowledge and to be able to act with authority in determining which term is sanctioned by the best usage, which is the most recent, which synonymous terms exist, hence require references, and what is the relationship, for the purpose of reference, of other headings in the catalog to the heading chosen.

Use of Outside Specialists. Few libraries require a large enough staff of catalogers to provide the amount of specialization required for establishing headings on the highest possible level of competence. Yet even libraries whose catalogers are not specialists in the subjects named above need not be satisfied to accept the lowest level of competence—the level represented by catalogers without any substantial knowledge of the subject, who must resort to extended, not always rewarding, searches in reference works, general treatises, and periodical literature. In college and university libraries the teaching and research staffs can provide the necessary special knowledge.

This knowledge cannot, however, always be used directly. The faculty specialist does not always know the principles on which the alphabetical subject catalog is constructed and must, consequently, be "indoctrinated." This indoctrination must include at least the following points:

1) Subject headings are predetermined and are independent of the terminology of the book in hand, being based on current American usage among competent authorities in the field.

2) The personal preferences of the specialist and his conception of the appropriateness of a term must yield to usage—in a scholarly library, the usage of the world of scholarship, and in a popular library, popular usage among educated people.

3) Headings must represent specifically the body of subject matter under consideration, and, therefore, use terminology as specific as the English language provides.

4) The form of the heading, in the case of headings consisting of more than one word, must take into account other similar or related headings in the catalog.

5) References to the heading adopted should be made from synonymous English terms in current American usage, in the book in hand, and, eventually, other books on the subject added to the library's collections.

6) References should be made from related headings already in the catalog which are broader than, and comprehend, the given heading, or are coordinate and possess a permanent, rather than an accidental, relationship to it, e. g., "see also" references from *Skull* to *Head* and *Brain* to *Head*, but not from *Hats* to *Head*.

7) References should be made from the heading adopted to headings already in the catalog which are narrower and are comprehended within it, as well as from related coordinate headings, provided the relationship is not accidental, e. g., "see also" references from *Head* to *Mouth* and *Head* to *Brain*, but not from *Head* to *Head-gear*.

Even so, the faculty specialist cannot be expected to know precisely which related headings requiring references are already in the catalog, nor, for that matter, to have sufficient knowledge of the accessions to the library's collections to advise the cataloger in regard to synonyms from which references to the chosen heading must eventually be made. Nevertheless, the knowledge of the specialist has to be relied on in the choice of terms and his judgment in regard to the propriety of proposed references, since, after all, it is he, among others, who must be served by means of the headings.[1]

---

[1] The position taken here is not invalidated by the view held by some librarians that a specialist, being abreast of the literature of his field, has no need of the subject approach, since he knows the works in the field by the names of their authors and by their titles. Specialists must, in any case, inevitably use the subject approach when they seek material outside their immediate fields of specialization.

892869—51——7

Authority File.   Bearing in mind that usage is, in the main, the decisive factor in the choice of subject headings, the cataloger must be aware of changing usage and continually bring the headings in the list and in the catalog up to date.   This is possible only if the cataloger maintains a complete record of the headings showing, for each, which references have been made from it to related headings, from other headings to it, and on what sources of information the choice of the heading is based.   To distinguish it from the lists of headings to which a cataloger might resort in choosing new headings, a list of headings and references limited to the catalogs of the library is often spoken of as a subject authority list or file.

The subject authority list will obviously resemble a general list in its principal features.   It will show under each heading:

1)   the coordinate related headings found in the catalog to which "see also" references have been made;

2)   the less comprehensive, subordinate headings to which "see also" references have been made;

3)   the broader, more comprehensive headings from which "see also" references have been made to the given heading;

4)   the coordinate related headings from which such "see also" references have been made;

5)   the synonymous terms, and, in general, terms equivalent to the given heading, from which "see" references have been made directing the reader to the chosen heading;

6)   scope notes defining the heading and distinguishing it from other headings, in those instances where one of two or more meanings of the term has been chosen for its use as a heading, or where a distinction must be drawn between the given heading and others closely related to it;

7)   the citation of appropriate sources in which the term to be used as a heading was sought, with an indication of the differences found;

8)   the citation of the work which occasioned the establishment of the new heading.

Many libraries depend upon a standard, generally accepted list of headings, checking in it the heading and references which they have used in their catalogs and inserting the headings and references which they have themselves developed or drawn from other sources.   Some libraries, on the other hand, though they depend on a standard list, prefer to keep on cards a list of the headings and references they have used.   This form of an authority list is almost inevitable, if the record of references made is to be kept complete against the possible need of changing headings and references.   Standard lists, for example, indicate methods of subdivision, but, for reasons of economy of space and facility in consultation, they avoid listing under each heading the subdivisions used.   However, some subdivisions require references applicable solely to a given heading followed by a given subdivision.   Changes in such headings accompanied by subdivisions become necessary at times.   The lack of a record of the references in such instances makes it difficult, if not impossible, to find and change the references and may result in the retention in the catalog of misleading references or blind ones leading nowhere.

Thus, for example, a list is likely to include the heading *Agriculture* with an indication that it may be subdivided by place, but not specifically the headings *Agriculture—France* or *Agriculture—Ukraine*. Yet in order to serve the needs of the reader who will seek information on the agriculture of France or the Ukraine under the name of the country, it is necessary to make reference to those headings from *France—Agriculture* and *Ukraine—Agriculture* and, by the same token, to maintain entries in an authority list on which the references might be traced. Obviously, authorities need be cited only for the main heading, except in those instances where the heading followed by the subdivision is used in lieu of a phrase heading for the purpose of fitting it into an existing pattern.

It is desirable that the authority card should as far as possible correspond in form to the list of headings which is mainly used by the library. The form of the entries in the fifth edition of *Subject Headings Used in the Dictionary Catalogs of the Library of Congress* is illustrated in the following example:

Offenses against property (Direct subdivision)

   sa   Arson; Burglary; Embezzlement; Extortion; Forcible entry
         and detainer; Forgery; Fraud; Larceny; Malicious mischief;
         Poaching; Receiving stolen goods; Robbery

   x   Crimes against property; Property, Crimes against; Prop-
        erty, Offenses against

  xx Criminal law

                                            ABC 25 May 1948

Face of authority card

Authorities:

  °Black

  ✓Bouvier (Offences against private property)

  ✓Wharton, Treatise on criminal law.   10th ed. 1896, v. 1, p. 618

Book cataloged: Gutiérrez Anzola, J. E.
Delitos contra la propiedad.   1944.

Back of authority card

Only the face of the card represents the entry in the list.   The symbols used have the following meanings:

    sa=make "see also" references to
    x=make "see" references from
    xx=make "see also" references from
    °=not found in authority cited
    ✓=found in authority cited; if form found differs from form used,
       form found is enclosed in parentheses following the citation.

The initials of the cataloger who established the heading, followed by the date, appear at the foot of the obverse of the card.

Authority cards prepared solely for the purpose of showing the references made need cite no authorities.   If a special form is used, it may bear the statement "For tracing references made."

The preparation of an authority card is but a first step.   The references from synonymous terms and the "see also" references must be checked against the list to make certain that the headings from which and to which they are to be made are actually in the catalog.   If an established heading is canceled or altered, not only must the authority card be canceled or revised accordingly, but new "see" references must be substituted for the old ones and the heading canceled or altered in all the "see also" references traced on the authority card.

In order to maintain a desirable degree of uniformity in the word pattern of headings and subdivisions, certain auxiliary records are required. The principal one is a list of subject subdivisions, each subdivision followed by the headings under which it has been used.[2]

It is useful also to maintain a list of the geographic names used either as main headings or as subdivisions, with indication of references from variant forms and related names and, where necessary, statements regarding distinctions between names and limitations on their use. As an example, Alsace-Lorraine and related place names may be cited:

Alsace-Lorraine.

> The united provinces of Alsace and Lorraine formed following the Treaty of Frankfurt in 1871.

> *sa* Alsace; Lorraine; Moselle, France (Dept.); Rhin, Bas-, France (Dept.); Rhin, Haut-, France (Dept.)

> *x* Elsass-Lothringen.

> *xx* Alsace; Lorraine.

Alsace.

> The old German province of Alsace (German: Elsass); upon the cession of Alsace-Lorraine to France in 1918 formed the French departments of Haut-Rhin and Bas-Rhin.

> *sa* Alsace-Lorraine; Rhin, Bas-, France (Dept.); Rhin, Haut-, France (Dept.)

> *x* Elsass.

> *xx* Alsace-Lorraine.

Lorraine.

> The region which in the Middle Ages formed the Kingdom of Lorraine (German: Lothringen); by the treaty of Frankfurt in 1871, parts of it formed, together with Alsace, the united provinces of Alsace-Lorraine; returned to France in 1918 to form the French department of Moselle; after the German occupation in 1940 was combined with the Saar territory to form the Westmark. Use *Lorraine* and *Saar Valley* as subject headings in lieu of *Westmark.*

> *sa* Alsace-Lorraine; Moselle, France (Dept.)

> *x* Lothringen.

> *xx* Alsace-Lorraine.

Moselle, France (Dept.)

> A department formed of part of the historic region of Lorraine; under the Treaty of Frankfurt, 1871, was ceded to Germany to form part of the united provinces of Alsace-Lorraine.

> *xx* Alsace-Lorraine; Lorraine.

---

[2] *Subject Subdivisions* published by the Library of Congress (6th ed.; 1924) is an example of this kind of auxiliary record.

Westmark.
>Formed after the German occupation in 1940 of the French department of the Moselle and the Saar territory. For subject entries use *Lorraine* and *Saar Valley* instead of *Westmark*.

Saar Valley.
>*Cf.* note under *Westmark*.

Rhin, Bas-, France (Dept.)
>Part of the territory of Alsace.

>*xx* Alsace; Alsace-Lorraine.

Rhin, Haut-, France (Dept.)
>Part of the territory of Alsace.

>*xx* Alsace; Alsace-Lorraine.

Qualifications of Cataloger. The application of subject headings to the materials acquired by the library requires the same degree of subject competence as the establishment of new headings. Therefore, a library whose collections lie for the greater part on the specialist's level of comprehension should attempt to attract specialists to that phase of the cataloging which must take into account the subject matter of the books. While even large libraries cannot afford such specialists in all fields of knowledge, and certainly not experts in limited fields, there are distinct advantages in having one or more specialists on the cataloging staff. In the first place, the specialist can do full justice to his own field of specialization; he can, moreover, deal more competently than the layman with related and peripheral fields. In the second place, the specialist is trained in methods of research, hence is more likely to test and check his results and can better understand other specialists to whom he must turn for areas outside his own. It can be successfully argued that, insofar as existing subject catalogs fail to serve adequately the purposes of research workers and specialists, the failure is due to the fact that they have in the main been created by educated laymen without special knowledge of the subjects with which they had to deal. It is probably true that, in all but a few special libraries, the cataloging is done by trained or experienced catalogers who lack an expert knowledge of the special subject to which the library is devoted.

In a special library the specialists who use it can, of course, generally be called on for help in cataloging. In some cases, especially when the library serves the research staff of a single industry or industrial concern, staff specialists can be assigned to assist in the cataloging. University libraries have the faculties to rely upon, while general reference libraries can sometimes make arrangements with specialists in the community to render necessary help to the library on some basis of reciprocity.

The knowledge of languages necessary in assigning subject headings differs only in degree from that required for other aspects of cataloging. Whereas, in determining the bibliographic facts with reference to a book, it is often possible to turn to authorities in other sources than those in the vernacular of the book, the cataloger who must assign the proper subject headings to it must possess in most instances not only a general knowledge of the language of the book, but also familiarity with the terminology of the subject. Lacking an adequate knowledge of a language, the cataloger can secure an adequate understanding of the book only by searching through encyclopedic works and language dictionaries in the subject and must check his findings carefully. If possible, he must seek out a specialist who knows the language of the book in order to corroborate his findings. Here, too, the cataloger who is expert in a particular field of knowledge must be given the opportunity to extend his linguistic competence in this field, since on it depends not only the quality of his work, but also his productive capacity.

Appendix A

GLOSSARY

Added entry. A secondary entry, *i. e.*, any entry other than the main entry. *Cf.* **Main entry.** There may be added entries for editor, translator, title, subjects, series, etc. Some catalogers would restrict the use of the term "added entry" to any entry other than the main entry and subject entries, using "secondary entry" as a group term to include all entries other than the main entry. Others would make the opposite choice, using "added entry" as the group term to include secondary entry and subject entry.

Alphabetical subject catalog. A catalog limited to subject entries and the necessary references, alphabetically arranged.

Alphabetico-classed catalog. A catalog with entries under broad subjects alphabetically arranged and subdivided by topics in alphabetical order.

Analytical subject entry. A subject entry for part of a work.

Anglo-American code (of cataloging). A term used for the rules of author and added entry compiled originally by committees of the American Library Association and the (British) Library Association and, in the main, representing the common practice of American and British libraries.

Anonymous classic. A work of unknown, doubtful, or supposedly supernatural authorship, which has appeared in the course of time in many editions, versions, and translations, and which is designated in the catalog by a fixed form of name, *i. e.*, the most commonly used, most distinctive, or first recorded title.

Author entry. Catalog entry under the name of the author or the heading which, under the rules for author entries, corresponds to it.

Author notation. *See* **Book number.**

Author number. *See* **Book number.**

Authority card. *See* **Subject authority card.**

"Black headings." Headings in a dictionary catalog other than subject headings. The term has its origin in the practice in many libraries of writing subject headings in red, others in black.

Book number. A symbol, usually consisting of a combination of letters and figures, which serves to identify a given book among others bearing the same class number and, at the same time, to place books bearing the same class number in the desired order on the shelves, by author, title, edition, and the

99

like. When used to arrange books alphabetically by author it is called "author number" or "author notation."

Card catalog. A catalog made up of cards, each usually bearing a single entry. The card catalog is to be distinguished from the printed catalog, in book form, and the sheaf catalog, which consists of sheets brought together in portfolios.

Catalogue raisonné. *See* **Classed catalog.**

Chronological subdivision. *See* **Period subdivision.**

Class catalog. *See* **Classed catalog.**

Class number. A symbol applied to a book indicating the class to which it belongs in the classification system used by the library. Together with the book number it forms the call number by which the location of the book on the shelf is indicated.

Classed catalog. A catalog arranged by subject according to a systematic scheme of classification. Also called "class catalog," "classified subject catalog," "systematic catalog," and *catalogue raisonné*.

Classification number. *See* **Class number.**

Classified subject catalog. *See* **Classed catalog.**

Composite work. A treatise on a single subject produced through the collaboration of two or more authors, the contribution of each forming a distinct section or part of the complete work.

Conventional title. A title by which a work is commonly known but which differs from the title under which it was published. It is used as a filing medium to bring all editions of the work together in the catalog. *Cf.* **Filing title.**

Corporate body. A group of individuals associated together as an organized unit, *e. g.*, a government, a government department, a society, an institution, a convention, a committee, a corporation.

Corporate name. The name of a corporate body as distinguished from the name of a person.

Dictionary catalog. A catalog, usually on cards, in which all the entries (author, title, subject, series, etc.) and their related references are arranged together in one general alphabet. The subarrangement frequently varies from the strictly alphabetical.

Direct and specific heading. *See* **Specific and direct heading.**

Direct subdivision. Subdivision of subject headings by name of province, county, city, or other locality without intermediate subdivision by name of country or state.

Double entry. *See* **Duplicate entry.**

Duplicate entry. Entry of the same subject matter under two distinct aspects of it, *e. g.*, *U. S.—Foreign relations—Gt. Brit.* and *Gt. Brit.—Foreign relations—U. S.* *Cf.* **Multiple entry.**

Entry. A record of a book in a catalog or list.

Entry word. The word by which an entry is arranged in a catalog or a bibliography, usually the first word of the heading. Also called "filing word."

Festschrift. A complimentary or memorial publication in the form of a collection of essays, addresses, or biographical, bibliographical, scientific, and other contributions, often embodying the results of research, issued in honor of a person, an institution, or a society, usually on the occasion of an anniversary celebration.

Filing title. The title of the work in the language in which it was originally written, or of the earliest edition, or of the author's manuscript of it, used as a filing medium for bringing all editions and translations of the work together in the catalog. *Cf.* **Conventional title.**

Filing word. *See* **Entry word.**

Form heading. A heading used for a form entry in a catalog, *e. g.*, *Encyclopedias and dictionaries, Periodicals, Short stories.* Sometimes known as "form subject heading." *Cf.* Charles A. Cutter, *Rules for a Dictionary Catalogue* (3d ed.; 1891), p. 13.

Form subdivision. A division of a subject heading based on form or arrangement of subject matter in books, as for dictionaries or periodicals.

Form subject heading. *See* **Form heading.**

General cross reference. *See* **General reference.**

General reference. A blanket reference in a catalog to the kind of heading under which one may expect to find entries for material on certain subjects or entries for particular kinds of names. Also called "general cross reference" and "information entry."

Geographic subdivision. *See* **Local subdivision.**

Guide-card. A card having a projecting, labeled edge or tab inserted in a file to indicate arrangement and to aid in locating material in the file.

Heading. In cataloging, the word, name, or phrase at the head of an entry to indicate some special aspect of the book (authorship, subject content, series, title, etc.) and thereby to bring together in the catalog associated and allied material.

Indirect subdivision. Subdivision of subject headings by name of country or state with further subdivision by name of province, county, city, or other locality.

Information entry. *See* **General reference.**

Language subdivision. A subdivision of a subject heading according to language, *e. g., English language—Dictionaries—French* for a dictionary of English words giving their French equivalents.

Local subdivision. Subdivision by the name of the geographic area to which the subject matter is limited.

Main entry. A full catalog entry, usually the author entry, giving all the information necessary to the complete identification of a work. In a card catalog this entry bears also the tracing of all the other headings under which the work in question is entered in the catalog. The main entry, used as a master card, may bear, in addition, the tracing of related references and a record of other pertinent official data concerning the work.

Multiple entry. Entry of the same subject under several headings, each representing a different approach. *Cf.* **Duplicate entry.**

Period subdivision. A subdivision of a subject heading which shows the period treated or during which the work appeared. Also called "time subdivision" and "chronological subdivision."

Place subdivision. *See* **Local subdivision.**

Qualified heading. A heading followed by a qualifying term which is usually enclosed in parentheses, *e. g., Bankruptcy (Canon law), Bankruptcy (International law), Dumping (Commercial policy), Escape (Ethics), Escape (Law), Composition (Law), Composition (Art), Composition (Music).*

"Refer from" reference. An indication, in a list of subject headings, of the headings from which references should be made to the given heading; it is the reverse of the indication of a "see" or "see also" reference.

Reference. A direction from one heading to another. *Cf.* **Subject reference.**

Relative index. An index to a classification system in which all relationships and aspects of the subject are brought together under each index entry.

Scope note. A statement indicating the scope of a subject heading and usually referring to related or overlapping headings.

"See also" reference. A reference to a less comprehensive or otherwise related term; the indication, in a list of subject headings, of such a reference.

"See" reference. A reference from a term or name under which no books are entered to that used in place of it; an indication, in a list of subject headings, of such a reference, that is, of the term or terms, synonymous with, or equivalent to, the given heading, to which a "see" reference is to be made.

Shelflist. A record of the books in the library arranged in the order in which they stand on the shelf, that is, in the order of their class and book numbers.

Specific and direct heading. A heading for a specific entry which expresses the topic directly, that is, one which is not preceded by the broad or class heading which includes it.

Specific entry. Entry of a book under a heading which expresses its special subject or topic as distinguished from the class or broad subject which includes that special subject or topic.

Specific heading. A heading which is no broader than the subject matter covered by it.

Subdivision. *See* **Subject subdivision.**

Subject. "The theme or themes of the book, whether stated in the title or not." (Cutter, p. 14.)

Subject analytic. *See* **Analytical subject entry.**

Subject authority card. A card which, in addition to citing the authorities consulted in determining the choice of a given heading, also indicates the references made to and from related headings and from synonymous terms.

Subject catalog. A catalog consisting of subject entries only.

Subject cross reference. *See* **Subject reference.**

Subject entry. An entry in a catalog or a bibliography under a heading which indicates the subject.

Subject-form heading. *See* **Form heading.**

Subject heading. A word or a group of words indicating a subject under which all material dealing with the same theme is entered in a catalog or a bibliography, or is arranged in a file.

Subject reference. A reference from one subject heading to another. Also called "subject cross reference." *Cf.* "Refer from" reference, "See" reference, "See also" reference.

Subject subdivision. The method of extending the subject heading by indicating the form of the subject matter, the place to which it is limited, or the part, element, or phase of the subject treated.

Syndetic. Having entries connected by cross references; said of a catalog.

Systematic catalog. *See* **Classed catalog.**

Time subdivision. *See* **Period subdivision.**

Title entry. The record of a work in a catalog or a bibliography under the title, generally beginning with the first word not an article. In a card catalog a title entry may be a main entry or an added entry.

Title page. A page at the beginning of a book or work, bearing its full title and usually, though not necessarily, the author's (editor's, etc.) name and the imprint. The leaf bearing the title page is commonly called the "title page," although properly it is the "title leaf."

Tracing.   In a card catalog, the record on the main entry card of all the additional headings under which the work is represented in the catalog.   Also, the record on a main entry card or on an authority card of all the related references made.   The tracing may be on the face or the back of the card, or on an accompanying card.

Unit card.   A basic catalog card, in the form of a main entry, which, when duplicated, may be used as a unit for all other entries for that work in the catalog by the addition of the appropriate heading.   Library of Congress printed cards are the most commonly used unit cards.

Appendix B

LIST OF CITIES IN THE UNITED STATES AND CANADA

for which the Library of Congress omits the designation of state or province [1]

Albany	Denver	Nashville	St. Paul
Annapolis	Des Moines	New Haven	Salt Lake City
Atlanta	Detroit	New Orleans	San Antonio
Atlantic City	Duluth	New York	San Francisco
Baltimore	Fort Wayne	Oklahoma City	Savannah
Boston	Grand Rapids	Omaha	Scranton
Brooklyn	Hartford	Ottawa	Seattle
Buffalo	Indianapolis	Philadelphia	Spokane
Chattanooga	Jersey City	Pittsburgh	Tacoma
Chicago	Los Angeles	Providence	Tallahassee
Cincinnati	Memphis	Quebec	Toledo
Cleveland	Milwaukee	Richmond	Toronto
Colorado Springs	Minneapolis	St. Augustine	Trenton
Dallas	Montreal	St. Louis	Wheeling

[1] In indirect subdivision by place the name of the state or province is nevertheless interpolated.

Appendix C

LIST OF CITIES OUTSIDE THE UNITED STATES AND CANADA

for which the Library of Congress omits the designation of country [1]

Aachen
Addis Ababa
Adelaide
Aleppo
Algiers (City)
Amsterdam
Ankara
Antwerp
Asunción
Athens
Augsburg
Bagdad
Baku
Barcelona
Basel
Beirut
Belfast
Belgrad
Berlin
Bern
Bogotá
Bologna
Bolzano (City)
[Also known as Bozen]
Bombay
Bonn
Bordeaux
Bratislava
[Also known as Pressburg]
Bremen
Brescia
Breslau

Brisbane
Brünn
[Also known as Brno]
Brunswick (City)
Brussels
Bucharest
Budapest
Buenos Aires
Cairo
Calcutta
Cape Town
Caracas
Ciudad Trujillo
[Also known as Santo Domingo]
Cluj
[Also known as Kolozsvár]
Coimbra
Cologne
Copenhagen
Cremona
Czernowitz
[Also known as Cernăuţi]
Damascus
Danzig
Delhi
Dresden
Dublin
Düsseldorf
Durazzo
Edinburgh

Erivan
Essen
Florence
Frankfurt am Main
Freiburg i. B.
Geneva
Genoa
Ghent
Glasgow
Graz
Guatemala (City)
Haarlem
Hague
Hamburg
Hanover (City)
Havana
Helsingfors
Istanbul
Jaffa
Jassy
Jerusalem
Johannesburg
Kaunas
[Also known as Kovno]
Kazan
Kharkov
Kiel
Kiev
Kishinev
Koblenz
Königsberg

Krakow
[Also known as Cracow]
Kyoto
Lahore
Leghorn
Leipzig
Lemberg
[Also known as Lwów]
Leningrad
[Also known as Petrograd and St. Petersburg]
Lhasa
Liége
Lille
Lima
Lisbon
Liverpool
London
Lübeck
Luxemburg (City)
Lyons
Madras
Madrid
Mainz
Managua
Manila
Maracaibo
Marseille
Melbourne
Mexico (City)

---

[1] In indirect subdivision by place the name of the country is nevertheless interpolated.

107

892869—51——8

Milan
Minsk
Monte Carlo
Montevideo
Moscow
Mosul
Munich
Nagasaki
Nancy
Naples
Nice
Nuremberg
    [Also known as
        Nürnberg]
Odessa
Osaka
Oslo
    [Also known as
        Christiania]
Oxford
Padua

Panama (City)
Paris
Peking
    [Also known as
        Peiping]
Prague
Pretoria
Quito
Rangoon
Reims
Reykjavik
Riga
Rio de Janeiro
Rome (City)
Rotterdam
Rouen
San Salvador
Santiago de Chile
Sevastopol
Seville
Shanghai

Smyrna
Sofia
Stalingrad
Stockholm
Strassburg
    [Also known as
        Strasbourg]
Stuttgart
Sydney
Tallinn
    [Also known as
        Reval]
Tartu
    [Also known as
        Dorpat]
Tashkend
Tegucigalpa
Teheran
Thessalonike
    [L. C. form; also
        known as Salo-
        niki]

Tokyo
Toulouse
Treves
    [Also known as
        Trier]
Tunis (City)
Turin
Uppsala
Utrecht
Valencia (City)
Valparaiso (City)
Venice
Vienna
Vilna
Warsaw
Wiesbaden
Zagreb
Zürich
Zutphen

Appendix D

GENERAL FORM SUBDIVISIONS

used in the Library of Congress catalogs under any subject heading as required [1]

Addresses, essays, lectures.
> For addresses, essays, or lectures, whether issued singly and dealing with the subject as a whole in general terms, or in collections by one or more authors dealing with various aspects or branches of a subject. The subdivision is not used for works to which the term "essay" is applied but which are in fact comprehensive treatises on a subject or a branch of a subject.

Bibliography.

Bio-bibliography.

Collected works.
> Ordinarily for works of one author. In certain cases, especially under scientific and technical subjects, the subdivision *Collected works* covers works by one or more authors, *e. g., Science—Collected works.*

Collections.
> Ordinarily to cover collections of works by different authors. However, in certain cases, especially under scientific and technical headings, the subdivision *Collected works* is used for works of either one or more authors in order to avoid conflict with headings for works on collections of objects, such as *Arms and armor—Collections, Autographs— Collections.*

Congresses.

Dictionaries.

Directories.

Exhibitions.

Handbooks, manuals, etc.

History.

Outlines, syllabi, etc.
> Confined to syllabi and outlines in the strict sense of these terms. Does not include treatises to which the terms compends, manuals, or handbooks are applied.

Periodicals.

Societies.
> For collections, memoirs, reports, transactions, etc., of societies under the name of the subject or subjects of which they treat, *e. g., Botany—Societies.*

Societies, etc.
> For publications of universities, museums, and other institutions, and of certain commissions which are not societies in the ordinary acceptation of the word.

---

[1] Under certain headings variations of these subdivisions are used.

Society publications.

> For works on subjects where the use of *Societies* would be ambiguous, *e. g.*, *Ants—Society publications, Fungi—Society publications, Insects—Society publications.*

Statistics.
Study and teaching.
Yearbooks.

Appendix E

LIST OF LOCAL DIVISIONS

which are always used in the Library of Congress catalogs as direct subdivisions

The following local divisions are exceptions to the general rule in regard to indirect subdivision; they are always used directly after the subject heading (*e. g.*, Agriculture—Alsace; Botany—Ohio; Education—Prussia; Fruit-culture—Ontario).

The States and territories of the United States; also District of Columbia, New York (City), and Washington, D. C.

The Provinces of Canada.

The States of Australia:
New South Wales; Queensland; South Australia; Tasmania; Victoria; Western Australia.

The States of Germany:
Anhalt; Baden; Bavaria; Bremen; Brunswick; Hamburg; Hesse; Lippe; Lübeck; Mecklenburg; Oldenburg; Prussia; Saxony; Schaumburg-Lippe; Thuringia; Württemberg.

The Provinces of Prussia:
Brandenburg; Grenzmark Posen-Westpreussen; Hanover; Hesse-Nassau; Hohenzollern; Pomerania; Prussia, East; Rhine Province; Saxony; Schleswig-Holstein; Silesia, Lower; Silesia, Upper; Westphalia.

The Provinces of Bavaria:
Bavaria, Lower; Bavaria, Upper; Franconia, Lower; Franconia, Middle; Franconia, Upper; Palatinate; Palatinate, Upper; Swabia.

The Provinces, etc., of Austria:
Austria, Lower; Austria, Upper; Burgenland; Carinthia; Salzburg; Styria; Tyrol; Vorarlberg.

The Provinces of the Netherlands:
Brabant, North; Drenthe; Friesland; Gelderland; Groningen; Holland, North; Holland, South; Limburg; Overijssel; Utrecht; Zealand.

Divisions of France:
Alsace; Angoumois; Anjou; Artois; Aunis; Auvergne; Béarn; Berry; Bourbonnais; Brittany; Burgundy; Champagne; Dauphiné; Flanders; Foix; Franche-Comté; Gascony; Guyenne; Ile de France (Province); Languedoc; Limousin; Lorraine; Lyonnais; Maine; Marche; Navarre; Nivernais; Normandy; Orléanais; Perche; Picardy; Poitou; Provence; Roussillon; Saintonge; Savoy; Touraine; also Corsica.

Divisions of Italy:

> Abruzzi and Molise; Apulia; Calabria; Campania; Emilia; Latium; Liguria; Lombardy; Lucania; Marches; Piedmont; Sardinia; Sicily; Tuscany; Umbria; Veneto; Venezia Giulia; Venezia Tridentina.

Besides the local divisions given above, subdivision of subject headings is direct to areas which in the course of their history have formed a part of more than one state; also to ecclesiastical provinces (archdioceses, dioceses, etc.) which do not fall wholly within, or are not identified with, one political jurisdiction.

Appendix F

ABBREVIATIONS

used in subject subdivisions in the Library of Congress catalogs

Antiquities	Antiq.
Bibliography	Bibl.
Bio-bibliography	Bio-bibl.
Biography	Biog.
Boundaries	Bound.
Commerce	Comm.
Description	Descr.
Description and travel	Descr. & trav.
Dictionaries and encyclopedias	Dict. & encyc.
Directories	Direct.
Discovery and exploration	Disc. & explor.
Economic conditions	Econ. condit.
Emigration and immigration	Emig. & immig.
Foreign relations	For. rel.
Genealogy	Geneal.
History	Hist.
History and criticism	Hist. & crit.
Industries	Indus.
Manufactures	Manuf.
Periodicals	Period.
Politics and government	Pol. & govt.
Sanitary affairs	Sanit. affairs
Social conditions	Soc. condit.
Social life and customs	Soc. life & cust.
Statistics	Stat.

The abbreviations Gt. Brit. and U. S. are used both as main headings and in subdivisions, except that neither is abbreviated when it stands alone without subdivision and Great Britain is not abbreviated in phrase headings, *e. g.*, Jews in Great Britain.

Appendix G

List of Subdivisions and References Used in Library of Congress Catalogs

Shakespeare, William, 1564–1616.
> Omit dates when used with subheading.

—Adaptations.

—Bibliography.

—Allusions.

—Ancestry. *See subdivision* Biography—Ancestry.

—Anniversaries, etc.
> Subdivided by date, *e. g.*, Shakespeare, William—Anniversaries, etc., 1916.
>
> *x subdivisions* Centennial celebrations, etc.; Exhibitions.

—Appreciation.

> —Armenia, [Europe, France, Germany, United States, U. S. —Philadelphia *(with a "see" reference from the subdivision* Appreciation—Philadelphia), etc.]

—Authorship.
> *x subdivision* Canon.

—Baconian theory.
> *sa* Bacon, Francis, viscount St. Albans—Cipher.
>
> *x* Bacon-Shakespeare controversy; Shakespeare-Bacon controversy.

> —Bibliography.

—Baconian theory (Con)

—Baconian theory (Pro)

—Collaboration.

—Dyer.

—Oxford theory.
> *xx* **Oxford, Edward De Vere**, *earl of*, 1550–1604.
>
> The Library of Congress enters works on the Oxford theory both under the above heading and the name of the Earl of Oxford

—Autographs.
> *sa subdivision* Manuscripts.
>
> *x subdivision* Handwriting.
>
> *xx subdivision* Manuscripts.

—Autographs, Spurious.

Shakespeare, William   *(Continued)*
—Bibliography.
    sa   Genée, Rudolf, 1824–1914—Bibliography; Rolfe, Wil-
       liam James, 1827–1910—Bibliography.
    x subdivisions Editions; Exhibitions.
—Folios.
—Folios. 1623.
—Folios. 1632.
—Quartos.
—Biography.
  —Ancestry.
    x   subdivision Ancestry.
  —As an actor.
    x   Shakespeare as an actor.
  —Character.
    x   subdivision Character.
  —Last years.
    x   subdivision Last years.
  —London life.
    x   subdivision London life.
  —Marriage.
    x   subdivision Marriage.
  —Sources.
    —Bibliography.
  —Youth.
    x   subdivision Youth.
—Birthday books.
—Calendars, etc.
—Canon. *See subdivisions* Authorship; Criticism, Textual.
—Centennial celebrations, etc. *See subdivision* Anniversaries, etc.
—Character. *See subdivision* Biography—Character.
—Characters.
  —Children.
  —Comic characters.
    x   subdivision Comic characters.
  —Criminals.
    x   subdivision Criminals.
    xx   Crime in literature.
  —Fairies.
  —Falstaff.
    x   Falstaff, *Sir* John.
  —Fathers.
  —Fools.

Shakespeare, William—Characters *(Continued)*
 —Ghosts.
  xx Ghosts in literature.
 —Iago.
 —Irish.
 —Jews.
  sa *subdivision* Characters—Shylock.
  xx Jews in literature.
 —Madmen.
  xx Insanity in literature.
 —Margaret of Anjou.
  xx **Margaret of Anjou**, *consort of Henry VI*, 1430–1482.
 —Rogues and vagabonds.
 —Shallow.
 —Shylock.
  sa Shylock.
  xx Shylock; *also subdivision* Characters—Jews.
 —Teachers.
  xx Teachers in literature.
 —Villains.
  x *subdivision* Villains.
  xx Crime in literature.
 —Welshmen.
 —Women.
  x *subdivision* Women.
  Example under Women in literature.
 —Chronology of the plays.
 —Comedies.
 —Comic characters. *See subdivision* Characters—Comic
  characters.
 —Concordances.
  sa *subdivision* Dictionaries, indexes, etc.
  Example under Concordances.
 —Contemporaries.
 —Contemporary England.
  xx England—Social life and customs—16th century.
 —Contemporary stage. *See subdivision* Stage history—To 1625.
 —Costume. *See subdivisions* Dramaturgy; Knowledge—
  Costume.
 —Criminals. *See subdivision* Characters—Criminals.
 —Criticism, Textual.
  x *subdivision* Canon.
  Example under Criticism, Textual.
 —Criticism and interpretation.

Shakespeare, William *(Continued)*
—Curiosa and miscellany.
    sa   *subdivision* Spiritualistic interpretations.
—Death mask.
—Dialects. *See subdivision* Language—Dialects.
—Dictionaries, indexes, etc.
    sa   *subdivision* Language—Glossaries, etc.
    xx   *subdivision* Concordances.
—Drama, fiction, etc. *See* Shakespeare in fiction, drama,
    poetry, etc.
—Dramaturgy.
    sa   *subdivision* Knowledge—Costume.
    x   *subdivisions* Costume; Stage-setting and scenery.
—Editions. *See subdivision* Bibliography.
—Editors.
—Exhibitions. *See subdivisions* Anniversaries, etc.;
    Bibliography.
—Family. *See* Shakespeare family.
—Fiction, drama, etc. *See* Shakespeare in fiction, drama,
    poetry, etc.
—Folk-lore, mythology.
    x   *subdivision* Mythology.
    xx   *subdivision* Knowledge and learning.
—Forgeries.
  —Collier.
        xx   **Collier, John Payne**, 1789–1883.
  —Ireland.
        xx   **Ireland, William Henry**, 1777–1835.
—Friends and associates.
—Glossaries, etc. *See subdivision* Language—Glossaries, etc.
—Grammar. *See subdivision* Language—Grammar.
—Grave.
—Handbooks, manuals, etc.
—Handwriting. *See subdivision* Autographs.
—Histories.
—Homes and haunts.
      Subdivided by place.
  —London.
        xx   London—Description.
  —Oxford.
        xx   Oxford—Description.
  —Stratford-upon-Avon.
        xx   Stratford-upon-Avon—Description.

Shakespeare, William *(Continued)*
—Humor.
—Iconography. *See subdivisions* Illustrations; Monuments,
    etc.; Museums, relics, etc.; Portraits, etc.
—Illustrations.
    x subdivision Iconography.
—Catalogs.
—Illustrations (Comic)
—Influence.
    —Pushkin, [Scott, Tieck, etc.]
        Added entry under the name of the writer influenced should be
          made.
—Knowledge.
    This heading, which occurs only with subdivision, is used for material
      dealing with Shakespeare's knowledge or treatment of specific
      subjects. Works on his learning and scholarship in general are
      entered under the subdivision Knowledge and learning.

—Animal lore. *See subdivision* Natural history.
—Archery.
—Art.
—Astrology.
—Astronomy.
—Bible.
—Birds. *See subdivision* Natural history.
—Classical literature.
—Costume.
    x subdivision Costume.
    xx subdivision Dramaturgy.
—Drinking.
—Dueling.
—Economics.
—Fishing.
—Flowers. *See subdivision* Natural history.
—Freemasons.
—Geography.
—Heraldry.
—History.
—Insanity.
—Italy.
—Language and languages.
—Latin literature.
—Law.
    x subdivision Legal knowledge.
—Medicine.

Shakespeare, William—Knowledge *(Continued)*
    —Military life.
    —Music. *See subdivision* Music.
    —Natural history. *See subdivision* Natural history.
    —Naval art and science.
    —Plant lore. *See subdivision* Natural history.
    —Precious stones.
    —Printing.
    —Psychology.
    —Science.
    —Sports.
—Knowledge and learning.
    cf. note under subdivision Knowledge.

    sa subdivisions Folk-lore, mythology; Music; Natural
        history; Philosophy; Political and social views; Religion
        and ethics.
    x subdivision Learning.
—Language.
    —Dialects.
        x subdivision Dialects.
    —Glossaries, etc.
        x subdivision Glossaries, etc.
        xx subdivision Dictionaries, indexes, etc.
    —Grammar.
        x subdivision Grammar.
    —Pronunciation.
        x subdivision Pronunciation.
    —Punctuation.
—Last years. *See subdivision* Biography—Last years.
—Learning. *See subdivision* Knowledge and learning.
—Legal knowledge. *See subdivision* Knowledge—Law.
—London life. *See subdivision* Biography—London life.
—Manuscripts.
    sa subdivision Autographs.
    xx subdivision Autographs.
—Marriage. *See subdivision* Biography—Marriage.
—Monuments, etc.
    x subdivision Iconography.
—Moving-pictures.
    Works on Shakespeare as he is represented in moving-pictures are
        entered under the heading Shakespeare in fiction, drama, poetry,
        etc.

Shakespeare, William *(Continued)*
—Museums, relics, etc.
    x subdivision Iconography.
—Music.
    x subdivisions Knowledge—Music; Songs.
    xx subdivision Knowledge and learning.
—Mythology. *See subdivision* Folklore, mythology.
—Name.
    Example under Names, Personal.
—Natural history.
    x subdivisions Knowledge—Animal lore; Knowledge—
      Birds; Knowledge—Flowers; Knowledge—Natural history;
      Knowledge—Plant lore.
    xx subdivision Knowledge and learning.
—Outlines, syllabi, etc. *See subdivision* Study—Outlines, syl-
    labi, etc.
—Pageants.
—Parodies, travesties, etc.
    Example under references from Comic literature; Literature,
      Comic.
—Patriotism.
—Periodicals. *See subdivision* Societies, periodicals, etc.
—Philosophy.
    xx subdivision Knowledge and learning.
—Plots.
—Poetry, fiction, etc. *See* Shakespeare in fiction, drama,
    poetry, etc.
—Political and social views.
    xx subdivision Knowledge and learning.
—Portraits, etc.
    x subdivision Iconography.
  —Catalogs.
—Pronunciation. *See subdivision* Language—Pronunciation.
—Prose.
—Quotations.
—Religion and ethics.
    xx subdivision Knowledge and learning.
—Signet-ring.
—Societies, periodicals, etc.
    x subdivisions Periodicals; Yearbooks.
—Songs. *See subdivision* Music.
—Sources.
  —Bibliography.

Shakespeare, William   *(Continued)*
  —Spiritualistic interpretations.
        xx   subdivision Curiosa and miscellany.
  —Spurious and doubtful works.   *See* **Shakespeare, William.**
        Spurious and doubtful works.
  —Stage history.
        sa **London.   Blackfriars Theatre.**
  —To 1625.
        x   subdivision Contemporary stage.
  —1625–1800.
  —1800–

  —France, [Germany, etc.]
  —Stage-setting and scenery.   *See subdivision* Dramaturgy.
  —Study.
    —History.
    —Outlines, syllabi, etc.
        x   subdivision Outlines, syllabi, etc.
  —Style.
  —Supernatural element.
        xx Supernatural in literature.
  —Technique.
  —Tragedies.
  —Translations.
  —Translations, French, [German, etc.]
  —Translators.
  —Versification.
  —Villains.   *See subdivision* Characters—Villains.
  —Will.
  —Women.   *See subdivision* Characters—Women.
  —Yearbooks.   *See subdivision* Societies, periodicals, etc.
  —Youth.   *See subdivision* Biography—Youth.
Shakespeare family.
      x Shakespeare, William—Family.
Shakespeare as an actor.   *See* Shakespeare, William—Biography—
      As an actor.
Shakespeare-Bacon controversy.   *See* Shakespeare, William—
      Authorship—Baconian theory.
Shakespeare in fiction, drama, poetry, etc.
      x Shakespeare, William—Drama, fiction, etc.; Shakespeare,
      William—Fiction, drama, etc.; Shakespeare, William—
      Poetry, fiction, etc.
                              *   *   *

The following headings are related to Shakespeare headings by means of references:

Bacon, Francis, viscount St. Albans.
—Cipher.
> Here are entered works relating to Bacon's cipher itself. Works relating to his authorship of Shakespeare's plays are entered under the heading Shakespeare—Authorship—Baconian theory.

Bacon-Shakespeare controversy. *See* Shakespeare, William—Authorship—Baconian theory.

Collier, John Payne, 1789–1883.
> *sa* Shakespeare, William—Forgeries—Collier.

Crime in literature.
> *sa* Shakespeare, William—Characters—Criminals; Shakespeare, William—Characters—Villains.

England.
—Social life and customs.
——16th century.
> *sa* Shakespeare, William—Contemporary England.

Falstaff, *Sir* John. *See* Shakespeare, William—Characters—Falstaff.

Genée, Rudolf, 1824–1914—Bibliography.
> *xx* Shakespeare, William—Bibliography.

Ghosts in literature.
> *sa* Shakespeare, William—Characters—Ghosts.

Insanity in literature.
> *sa* Shakespeare, William—Characters—Madmen.

Ireland, William Henry, 1777–1835.
> *sa* Shakespeare, William—Forgeries—Ireland.

Jews in literature.
> *sa* Shakespeare, William—Characters—Jews.

London.
—Description.
> *sa* Shakespeare, William—Homes and haunts—London.

London. Blackfriars Theatre.
> *xx* Shakespeare, William—Stage history.

Margaret of Anjou, *consort of Henry VI,* 1430–1482.
> *sa* Shakespeare, William—Characters—Margaret of Anjou.

Oxford, Edward De Vere, *earl of,* 1550–1604.
> *sa* Shakespeare, William—Authorship—Oxford theory.

Oxford.
—Description.
> *sa* Shakespeare, William—Homes and haunts—Oxford.

Rolfe, William James, 1827–1910—Bibliography.
> *xx* Shakespeare, William—Bibliography.

Shylock.

>   *sa*   Shakespeare, William—Characters—Shylock.
>
>   Here are entered works in which the character Shylock occurs or works
>   about the character. Works relating to the Shylock of Shake-
>   speare's Merchant of Venice are entered under the heading Shake-
>   speare, William—Characters—Shylock.

Stratford-upon-Avon.

—Description.

>   *sa*   Shakespeare, William—Homes and haunts—Strat-
>   ford-upon-Avon.

Supernatural in literature.

>   *sa*   Shakespeare, William—Supernatural element.

Teachers in literature.

>   *sa*   Shakespeare, William—Characters—Teachers.

LINCOLN

List of Subdivisions and References Used in Library of Congress Catalogs

Lincoln, Abraham, Pres. U. S., 1809–1865.

>   Omit dates when used with subheading.
>
>   *sa*   Lincoln-Douglas debates, 1858.

—Addresses, sermons, etc.

>   *sa*   *subdivision* Anniversaries, etc.

—Anecdotes.

>   *Example under* Anecdotes.

—Anniversaries, etc.

>   *sa*   *subdivision* Memorial services.
>
>   *x*   *subdivision* Centennial celebrations.
>
>   *xx*   *subdivision* Addresses, sermons, etc.

—As a lawyer.

>   *x*   Lincoln as a lawyer; *also subdivision* Law practice.

—Assassination.

>   *sa*   **Booth, John Wilkes, 1838–1865; Surratt, John Harrison,**
>   **1844–1916; Surratt, Mary Eugenia (Jenkins) 1820–1865.**

—Bibliography.

—Autographs.

>   *x*   *subdivision* Handwriting.

—Bibliography.

>   *x*   *subdivision* Lincolniana.

—Birthplace.

>   *sa*   **Abraham Lincoln National Historical Park.**
>
>   *xx*   *subdivision* Homes.

—Books and reading.

Lincoln, Abraham, Pres. U. S. *(Continued)*
—Cartoons, satire, etc.
    Example under Caricatures and cartoons.
—Centennial celebrations. *See subdivision* Anniversaries, etc.
—Debates with Douglas, 1858. *See* Lincoln-Douglas debates, 1858.
—Drama.
—Family.
—Fiction.
—Funeral journey to Springfield.
—Funeral services.
—Handwriting. *See subdivision* Autographs.
—Homes.
    sa **Springfield, Ill. Lincoln Home;** *also subdivision* Birthplace.
—Iconography.
—Inauguration.
—Journey to Washington, Feb. 1861.
—Juvenile literature.
—Law practice. *See subdivision* As a lawyer.
—Lincolniana. *See subdivisions* Bibliography; Museums, relics, etc.
—Literary art.
—Manuscripts.
  —Facsimiles.
—Medals.
    Example under Medals.
—Memorial services.
    xx subdivision **Anniversaries, etc.**
—Monuments, etc.
    sa entries for individual monuments (statues, memorial buildings and parks, etc.), e. g., **Cincinnati. Lincoln Statue; Edinburgh. Lincoln Monument; Lincoln Pioneer Village, Rockport, Ind.; Nancy Hanks Lincoln Memorial and Lincoln State Park, Indiana.**
—Museums, relics, etc.
    sa **Lincoln Museum, Washington, D. C.; Oldroyd Collection of Lincoln Relics.**
    x subdivisions Lincolniana; Relics.
—Music. *See subdivision* Songs and music.
—Personality.
—Poetry.
—Political career before 1861.

Lincoln, Abraham, Pres. U. S.   (*Continued*)
—Portraits.
—Relations with Jews.
—Relics.   *See subdivision* Museums, relics, etc.
—Religion.
—Songs and music.
  x *subdivision* Music.
—Tomb.
  sa **Lincoln Guard of Honor.**
  x **Springfield, Ill.   Lincoln Monument.**
—Views on slavery.
—Views on temperance.

*   *   *

The following headings are related to Lincoln headings by means of references:

Abraham Lincoln National Historical Park.
  xx Lincoln, Abraham, Pres. U. S.—Birthplace.
Booth, John Wilkes, 1838–1865.
  xx Lincoln, Abraham, Pres. U. S.—Assassination.
Lincoln, Abraham, *Pres. U. S.,* 1809–1865.
  [Lincoln-Douglas debates]
  Works about the Lincoln-Douglas debates are entered under the heading Lincoln-Douglas debates, 1858.
Lincoln as a lawyer.   *See* Lincoln, Abraham, Pres. U. S.—As a lawyer.
Lincoln-Douglas debates, 1858.
  The text of the Lincoln-Douglas debates is entered under the heading **Lincoln, Abraham,** *Pres. U. S.,* 1809–1865. [Lincoln-Douglas debates]
  x Lincoln, Abraham, Pres. U. S.—Debates with Douglas, 1858.
  xx Lincoln, Abraham, Pres. U. S., 1809–1865.
Lincoln Guard of Honor.
  xx Lincoln, Abraham, Pres. U. S.—Tomb.
Springfield, Ill.   Lincoln Home.
  xx Lincoln, Abraham, Pres. U. S.—Homes.
Springfield, Ill.   Lincoln Monument.   *See* Lincoln, Abraham, Pres. U. S.—Tomb.
Surratt, John Harrison, 1844–1916.
  xx Lincoln, Abraham, Pres. U. S.—Assassination.
Surratt, Mary Eugenia (Jenkins) 1820–1865.
  xx Lincoln, Abraham, Pres. U. S.—Assassination.

Index